WORLD BANK STAFF WORKING PAPERS
Number 585

MANAGEMENT AND DEVELOPMENT SERIES
Number 12

Successes and Failures in Meeting the Management Challenge

Strategies and Their Implementation

Milan Kubr
John Wallace

The World Bank
Washington, D.C., U.S.A.

Copyright © 1983
The International Bank for Reconstruction
and Development / THE WORLD BANK
1818 H Street, N.W.
Washington, D.C. 20433, U.S.A.

First printing July 1983
Second printing July 1984

This is a working document published informally by the World Bank. To present the results of research with the least possible delay, the typescript has not been prepared in accordance with the procedures appropriate to formal printed texts, and the World Bank accepts no responsibility for errors. The publication is supplied at a token charge to defray part of the cost of manufacture and distribution.

The views and interpretations in this document are those of the author(s) and should not be attributed to the World Bank, to its affiliated organizations, or to any individual acting on their behalf. Any maps used have been prepared solely for the convenience of the readers; the denominations used and the boundaries shown do not imply, on the part of the World Bank and its affiliates, any judgment on the legal status of any territory or any endorsement or acceptance of such boundaries.

The full range of World Bank publications is described in the *Catalog of World Bank Publications*; the continuing research program of the Bank is outlined in *World Bank Research Program: Abstracts of Current Studies*. Both booklets are updated annually; the most recent edition of each is available without charge from the Publications Distribution Unit of the Bank in Washington or from the European Office of the Bank, 66, avenue d'Iéna, 75116 Paris, France.

Milan Kubr is chief of the Management Development Branch and John Wallace works for the Research and Program Development Unit, both at the International Labour Office, Geneva.

Library of Congress Cataloging in Publication Data

Kubr, Milan.
   Successes and failures in meeting the management challenge.

   (World Bank staff working papers ; no. 585.
Management and development subseries ; no. 12)
   Bibliography: p.
   1. Management--Developing countries. 2. Executives--
Training of--Developing countries. I. Wallace, John,
1939-   . II. Title. III. Series: World Bank staff
working papers ; no. 585. IV. Series: World Bank
staff working papers. Management and development subseries ; no. 12.
HD70.D44K82   1983   658.4'07124'091724   83-17061
ISBN 0-8213-0254-X

Foreword

This study is one in a series of World Bank Staff Working Papers devoted to issues of development management. Prepared as background papers for the World Development Report 1983, they provide an in-depth treatment of the subjects dealt with in Part II of the Report. The thirteen papers cover topics ranging from comprehensive surveys of management issues in different types of public sector institutions (for example, state-owned enterprises, the public service, and local government agencies) to broad overviews of such subjects as planning, management training, technical assistance, corruption, and decentralization.

The central concern underlying these papers is the search for greater efficiency in setting and pursuing development goals. The papers focus on the role of the state in this process, stress the importance of appropriate incentives, and assess the effectiveness of alternative institutional arrangements. They offer no general prescriptions, as the developing countries are too diverse--politically, culturally, and in economic resources-- to allow the definition of a single strategy.

The papers draw extensively on the experiences of the World Bank and other international agencies. They were reviewed by a wide range of readership from developing and developed countries inside and outside the Bank. They were edited by Victoria Macintyre. Rhoda Blade-Charest, Banjonglak Duangrat, Jaunianne Fawkes, and Carlina Jones prepared the manuscripts for publication.

I hope that these studies will be useful to practitioners and academicians of development management around the world.

Pierre Landell-Mills
Staff Director
World Development Report 1983

Papers in the Management and Development Series

1. Agarwala, Ramgopal. Price Distortions and Growth in Developing Countries. World Bank Staff Working Paper no. 575.

2. Agarwala, Ramgopal. Planning in Developing Countries: Lessons of Experience. World Bank Staff Working Paper no. 576.

3. Cochrane, Glynn. Policies for Strengthening Local Government in Developing Countries. World Bank Staff Working Paper no. 582.

4. Gordon, David. Development Finance Companies, State and Privately Owned: A Review. World Bank Staff Working Paper no. 578.

5. Gould, David J., and Jose A. Amaro-Reyes. The Effects of Corruption on Administrative Performance: Illustrations from Developing Countries. World Bank Staff Working Paper no. 580.

6. Knight, Peter T. Economic Reform in Socialist Countries: The Experiences of China, Hungary, Romania, and Yugoslavia. World Bank Staff Working Paper no. 579.

7. Kubr, Milan, and John Wallace. Successes and Failures in Meeting the Management Challenge: Strategies and Their Implementation. World Bank Staff Working Paper no. 585.

8. Lethem, Francis J., and Lauren Cooper. Managing Project-Related Technical Assistance: The Lessons of Success. World Bank Staff Working Paper no. 586.

9. Ozgediz, Selcuk. Managing the Public Service in Developing Countries: Issues and Prospects. World Bank Staff Working Paper no. 583.

10. Paul, Samuel. Training for Public Administration and Management in Developing Countries: A Review. World Bank Staff Working Paper no. 584.

11. Rondinelli, Dennis A., John R. Nellis, and G. Shabbir Cheema. Decentralization in Developing Countries: A Review of Recent Experience. World Bank Staff Working Paper no. 581.

12. Shinohara, Miyohei, Toru Yanagihara, and Kwang Suk Kim. The Japanese and Korean Experiences in Managing Development. Ed. Ramgopal Agarwala. World Bank Staff Working Paper no. 574.

13. Shirley, Mary M. Managing State-Owned Enterprises. World Bank Staff Working Paper no. 577.

Table of Contents

Acronyms

BEDU	Bostwana Enterprise Development Unit
CEMIG	Centrais Electricas de Minas Gerais (Brazil)
CMD	Centre for Management Development (Nigeria)
EDP	Entrepreneurship Development Programme (Gujarat State, India)
GBHC	Ghana Bank for Housing and Construction
IFT	Instructor-free training
LWUA	Local Water Utilities Administration (Philippines)
MATCOM	Materials and techniques for cooperative management training
MDRS	Management Development Referral Service
NEPA	Nigerian Electricity Power Authority
NIBM	National Institute of Business Management (Sri Lanka)
NPC	National Productivity Centre (Ethiopia)
PIP	Programming (or planning) for improved enterprise performance
SEDCO	Small Enterprise Development Company (Swaziland)
TCDC	Technical cooperation among the Developing Countries

SUMMARY

Whatever development model is chosen, the quality of management will largely determine what is really achieved. This paper, based on the experience of the ILO Management Development Programme over the last thirty years and on that of many other organizations, reviews some important achievements and problems in meeting this challenge. The discussion falls into three parts: the first examines the origin and nature of key management problems currently faced by the developing countries; the second reviews the main strategies used by developing countries to improve management competence and performance; and the third looks at some promising approaches recently introduced by enterprises and institutions in the hope of making management development more effective.

The Management Challenge

Since management of both private and public organizations has had a short history in developing countries, its performance and effectiveness could not, on the whole, reach the standards attained by most industrialized countries. However, efforts to improve management in all sectors and at all levels need to be considerably increased. This requirement reflects (i) the growing international interdependence of economies and cultures, and (ii) the magnitude of internal development problems of developing countries, particularly in the rural and social sectors. Efforts to improve management need strong political support.

Strategies For Meeting The Challenge

As a rule, developing countries do not have comprehensive national strategies for improving management standards over a distinct period of time. However, a number of strategic choices have been made and followed by many such countries. Eight important strategies are examined in this part of the paper.

Role Assigned to Public Management.

In most developing countries, an important part of national development is handled by the public sector. In these countries a need arose to build a strong public administration of a new type, able to lead the country's development endeavor. For various reasons, a large number of public enterprises were established. The central problem in improving the management of public enterprises is that the basic approach to this improvement is not managerial and business-like, but administrative and bureaucratic. In addition, these countries need to improve performance from within the enterprises first of all; the inertia of public administration systems and conservative civil service attitudes often block management improvement efforts started by the central government.

Role Assigned to Private Management and Entrepreneurship.

The history of management is linked to the history of private enterprise. In many developing countries, the earlier mistrust of private enterprise is giving way to a pragmatic approach directed toward the mobilization of private initiative, resources, and management talent for national development. In particular, these countries need to create favourable conditions for entrepreneurship and for establishing new indigenous enterprises. This is a very slow process in least developed countries that have limited enterpreneurial tradition and experience. The role of education and national culture in promoting entrepreneurial attitudes and behaviors should be increased. Multinational corporations active in developing countries contribute to the enhancement of the managerial capabilities of these countries, but this contribution could be increased and oriented more towards national priorities.

Interaction Between Public and Private Management

Since most developing countries have mixed economies, there is great scope for sharing management experience and for innovation in promoting and organizing cooperation of the two sectors. Some examples, are mixed enterprises, joint ventures, or the contracting of various public services to small and medium private enterprises.

Strategy for Localizing Management

This strategy is followed by all developing countries in which foreign managers were needed after independence and in which they are still needed owing to shortages of local high-level manpower. There are differences between countries, as there are between corporations pursuing their specific localization objectives. On-the-job training has been the main method of training the new local managers replacing expatriates, but often it has not been systematic and has suffered from excessive staff turnover, brain drain, and management styles that hamper initiative and learning.

Transfer of Management Expertise from Industrialized Countries

This strategy is pursued by all developing countries, but in varying degrees. They also differ in their choice of the source of expertise. Considerable benefits have been drawn from transfer, but adaptation to local culture and the development of original local techniques and systems have been seriously neglected.

Building of Professional Institutions and Services to Management

The institution-building strategy has supplemented and accelerated on-the-job learning of management skills in both the public and private sectors. The growth of national institutions has been impressive and represents a major investment. In general, there is some merit in making institutions more effective, strengthening their links with the client base, increasing the practical usefulness of their programs, improving their coordination, and enchancing autonomy and responsibility for results. This effort requires a fundamental change of attitude and thinking in many institutions, which are supposed to promote effectiveness, productivity, and business-like behavior, but which are structured and behave like public bureaucracies.

Priority Given to the Modern Economic Sector

Until recently, the modern economic sector attracted most of the managerial manpower and resources allocated to management development. Management institutions are designed, too, to serve primarily the modern sector. This strategy is changing, but this change should be accelerated and should include the development of appropriate methods, as well as managers committed to social and rural development. This task should have high priority in the endeavor to overcome the current dichotomy of the modern and traditional sectors.

Role of Technical Cooperation

Technical cooperation has helped to build up managerial capabilities in developing countries. It has influenced both strategic choices and the implementation of strategies. Lessons from technical cooperation show that it needs to be better coordinated so that the staff development dimension of every project can be enhanced, less costly forms of cooperation can be used, and better use can be made of technical cooperation among the developing countries (TCDC).

The designers of management development strategies for future years should take the following steps: undertake self-appraisal exercises periodically to assess the state of management in a country; focus on priority sectors and harmonization of sectoral efforts; use a tripartite approach based on collaboration of government, business, and workers' and social organizations; coordinate and rationalize institutional networks; be dynamic, creative, and flexible in preparing managers to cope with future challenges.

Management Development: Some Promising Approaches

Many approaches to making management development more effective have been tried. They need to be examined, evaluated, and disseminated more systematically.

Interventions to Improve Management in Organizations

The ultimate goal of management development is to nudge organizations toward their own vision of excellence. Whether an approach is promising can be evaluated by means of a framework that links learning and behavioral change to organizational improvement from one period to the next. The approaches described in this section are less common than they need to be because too little evaluation is done, and consequently too few managers are aware of the power of management development. Several examples of superior organizations in developing countries show that such organizations invest in their managers through in-house and open programs. One promising approach to accelerate the acceptance of this type of investment is top management action planning. If used with several organizations, it can help overcome barriers that are often placed in the path of enterprises. Action planning approaches fail, however, when management teams lack the enthusiasm to implement the plans they committed themselves to and when the management institutions fail to support the efforts long enough.

Innovations in Management Education and Training

Such innovations are urgently needed in developing countries. One way to obtain the commitment of both the management institutions and the enterprises is to mount long-term campaigns designed to achieve specific goals in areas such as equipment maintenance, product quality and cost, and so forth. The problem is to reduce the cost of such interventions, spreading their availability and improving their impact. Many new products and services that show promise in this respect are invading the field of management development. Modular programs, for example, promise to reduce the cost of developing courses and campaigns designed on the basis of the best materials that exist. These can be tailored to local conditions by producing local case studies and other exercises and incorporating these into the modular packages. When managers from similar organizations meet in business clinics and compare their performance indicators, they often come up with suggestion for improving both their own performance and that of the whole group. This process of self-diagnosis, learning, and action planning can be brought to the level of individual managers through self-development systems. In many countries these have been combined with on-the-job projects in other organizations in what is known as "action learning." Electronic aids such as video-taped role playing and computer-based games and simulations are now being used in developing countries, especially in the programs that multinational firms use for their own managers. Such aids are expensive to produce and validate, and require reliable facilities that many countries still lack, especially in areas outside large urban centers.

Trends in Entrepreneurship Development

Entrepreneurship is vital to economic development, but few approaches have been shown to accelerate the development of entrepreneurs and to be cost effective. Entrepreneurs must be taught how to organize so that their common priority needs can be more efficiently met. In the construction sector, for example, an increasing number of countries are trying these approaches to help contractors. Services that help entrepreneurs to develop confidence, select good opportunities, and then survive are by no means common. Programs that help youth and artisans find opportunities for self-employment show some promise.

How to Make the Effective Approaches More Common

Serious evaluation, combined with widespread dissemination of information on successful techniques, is increasing. It appears that the best approaches will be widely used only where the management development professionals have the incentive to develop and apply the more powerful techniques that are available in partnership with managers who have the resources and the vision to strive for excellence. Management institutions should be helped in this endeavor.

I. Introduction

Since views differ on which development model is best, countries take different paths. They assign different roles to industrialization, domestic savings, foreign capital, central planning, imported technololgy, land reform, modernization of agriculture, public or private enterprise, large or small enterprise, and so on. Despite this diversity, developing countries--as well as agencies and business corporations acting as their foreign development partners--agree that the quality of management largely determines what is achieved. This unanimity is not based on any theory or ideology, but on experience. Improperly managed, even massive injections of finance and material resources, as well as superhuman efforts, produce only fleeting improvements.

This observation is not new. Much has been said and written about management in developing countries and about the management challenge they face. Much has been done to increase the number of competent local managers, to build and strengthen management institutions, to learn from countries possessing considerable management experience, and to spread the gospel of managerial effectiveness, productivity, and performance as widely as possible.

Yet the task is not complete. Perhaps the time has been too short and the effort inadequate. Errors, too, have been made. Meanwhile, requirements and conditions have evolved--the management challenge of the 1980s is not what it was thirty or even ten years ago. In 1960, for example, no one could have imagined the impact of the international financial system on management in developing countries in 1983. No one could have anticipated the spectacular changes in computer and communication technology and the new opportunities for utilizing them in Third World countries.

This paper, based on the experience of the International Labour Organisation's (ILO) Management Development Programme over the last thirty years, and on that of many other organizations and agencies with which this Programme cooperates, reviews some important achievements and problems in meeting the management challenge faced by the developing countries. It focuses on management development and on the management of enterprises, public and private. Since enterprises are managed in a wider context of national and even international economics, however, the paper also touches upon certain institutional and management issues exceeding the framework of single enterprises.

The paper has three parts: the first briefly discusses the nature of management problems faced by the developing countries at the present time; the second part identifies and reviews the principal strategies used by most developing countries to increase their managerial capabilities and to improve the standards of management at various levels and in various sectors; the third looks in detail at some promising approaches that have been successfully used to train managers, increase organizational performance, and make institutional services to management more relevant and effective.

II. The Management Challenge

Emergence of Modern Management

Management, as it is understood in industrialized economies, is a recent phenomemon in developing countries. It emerged with the creation of complex organizations, projects, and programs: in industrial and commercial enterprises in the modern sector of the economy, in infrastructure development projects, in important social programs (for example, in education or public health), and in government agencies whose purpose is to promote and coordinate development.

Management in developing countries, of course, has older roots. Indeed, a limited number of large commercial and other enterprises existed in many regions of Africa, Asia, and Latin America during the colonial era, when plantations, mining companies, and a few manufacturing plants were established. Colonial administrations operated agencies for various types of services. Such organizations needed management. Most were managed by foreigners, however, the native population being admitted to supervisory and lower level positions at best. These organizations constituted foreign enclaves in traditional rural societies and their contribution to building local management expertise and culture was negligible. Many even followed an explicit policy of excluding the indigenous population from gaining competence in administration and management.

As well, there were some small enterprises owned and run by indigenous people. These engaged in trade, handicrafts, or manufacturing (for example, textile and shoes) and used rather primitive technology. Although they were based on, and in turn encouraged, local entrepreneurial talent, most were operated as family businesses with rudimentary management structures and systems.

Even the traditional societies that existed mostly as subsistence economies--they engaged mainly in primitive farming, cattle breeding, and hunting--had their particular social organization and social leaders who often enjoyed rights and responsibilities over work organization and controlled the pooling and use of productive resources, the distribution of the product of collective activity, and the like. The salient feature of the development path chosen after independence, however, is that it tended to implant a new economic and social structure intended to displace or control the traditional structures. The possibility of using traditional organizations and leaders for new types of economic activity and social services was largely unexplored; traditional social structures attracted anthropologists but not industrialists and politicians.

The history of management in developing countries is therefore not long--rarely more than twenty to thirty years old. Also, the managerial class in these countries is young--its average age and number of years of managerial experience are much below the levels of industrialized countries.

Is There a Management Gap?

The term "management gap" is often used to succinctly characterize the current state of management in developing countries by comparing it to management in industrialized countries. This concept covers the number, education, practical experience, and competence of managers; the techniques and systems used; and the performance and effectiveness achieved. In current usage, the term implies that Third World countries, on the whole, manage less effectively, even if they already have individuals and organizations whose performance is high by any standard.

But are such comparison valid and useful? Is it abnormal for developing countries to have different and lower standards of mangement and administration? Why compare them to the industrialized world? It has taken Europe and North America centuries to attain their present standards; and even today their management is much under attack, from various positions and for various reasons: for degrading the environment, for wasting scarce resources, for dehumanizing factor work, for lacking imagination and dynamism in creating new employment opportunities, and so on. Is it therefore an appropriate model to follow and replicate? After all, management is a social category, a mix of

skills, attitudes, behaviors, techniques, structures, and processes, which
never exists in a vacuum and always mirrors the material life, the production
methods, the social institutions, and the culture in any society. Flawless
management exists nowhere and it is only a dream in societies struck by
massive poverty, malnutrition, illiteracy, and other plagues of
underdevelopment.

Thus business and public management in industrialized countries does
not automatically provide models that should be followed blindly by the rest
of the world. Ideally, every country, or groups of countries, or large social
communities sharing similar problems should be able to develop and apply
management and administrative systems reflecting their particular economic and
sociocultural setting. In the contemporary world, however, no country does
this in isolation. Nobody is starting from scratch. The need to compare
management internationally, particularly in industrialized and developing
countries, and to draw from the management expertise available in other
countries, is imposed by the realities of our world.

Growing Interdependence

Management, then, is being affected by the growing interdependence of
economies and cultures: "Tightened economic linkages between nations make it
virtually impossible for any individual national government today to manage
its economy independently or to quarantine inflation ... The economic shell of
the nation-state is now increasingly permeable." 1/ In exports of
manufactured good, for example, the international market requires competitive
standards of design, quality, delivery conditions, after-sales servicing, and
price. To meet these standards countries must promote good planning,
coordination, productivity, and efficiency in the whole production and
distribution process. For the time being, poor management and low

productivity can, in many countries, be compensated for by extremely low wages; but for how long? Many developing countries, on the other hand, are keen to attract more foreign private capital to finance their development projects. But foreign investors hate to see their money mismanaged and give priority to those developing countries--and within developing countries to organizations and even individuals--that guarantee adequate standards of mangement and performance.

Technology--through its massive transfer from country to country and the unprecedented pace of technological change--has also increased managerial interdependence. The acquisition of particular technologies dictates the acquisition of corresponding management systems, at least their key elements. An electric power plant or an oil refinery places certain requirements on management that must be strictly observed. Transport, communication, and data processing technologies have created strong interlinkages between countries, and their future impact on both national and international management is likely to be greater than most of us can now imagine. It has been estimated that 90 percent of the technological developments currently in use have taken place within the last thirty years. No one is able to forecast, even roughly, how many of these developments will still be in use in the year 2000, and what new technologies will be available for large-scale practical application at prices that will make them fully accessible to developing countries.

A Dual Economy Context

The growing interdependence of nations affects management differently in different countries. The open economies of rapidly industrializing countries such as Korea, Singapore, or Brazil are directly exposed to the influence of international business and must be fairly adaptable and competitive. In predominantly agricultural countries with large internal markets and limited external economic relations, such as China, internal demands on management improvement are more important than external influences. Wherever these demands are low, improvements come slowly. Most developing countries contend with both influences. India, for example, is now a major exporter of manufactured goods, but more than 60 percent of its population is still living below the threshold of absolute poverty. The growing cost and scarcity of energy are also forcing developing countries to improve their management techniques. Any vital resource that rises in price because of growing scarcity creates new problems and places new demands on management.

A serious problem in most developing countries is the "dual" nature of their economies. Because of the growing interdependence of nations, management in the modern sector and government administration is forced to become even more similar to management in industrialized countries. At the same time, the traditional rural and urban economy is changing very slowly and benefits little from the growing expertise of the modern sector. The management gap is thus also becoming an internal, national phenomenon in that a wide gap now exists between the management of the modern sector and that of the traditional, predominantly rural, economy. At present, the developing countries stand with one leg in the modern economy, and in international trade circuits and money markets, often demonstrating high competence in making complex managerial, commercial, and financial decisions. With the other leg, they stand in a vast traditional economy—the development of which is still much neglected—where techniques and behavioral patterns have changed little over centuries.

Essence of the Management Challenge

In summary, the management challenge evolves along with the development challenge. To appreciate its existence and magnitude means to recognize that better management in all sectors and at all levels can accelerate development and make sure that development projects and programs will be designed and implemented more effectively. The improvement of management in developing countries is a necessity. It is dictated by the increasing interdependence of the world economy and by the internal economic and social forces in developing countries; in particular, it is necessary to enhance the contribution of management to developmental efforts in the traditional sectors and to reduce their relative lag behind the modern sector.

The management challenge has both a techniical and a sociopolitical dimension. From a strictly technical point of view, it can be described as a set of specific objectives, targets, actions, and programs that, if implemented, will generally raise the management standards in a country. The sociopolitical dimension is equally important. Substantial improvements in management and administration cannot be achieved without a strong will, commitment and direct guidance of the country's political leadership, and the full support of all social groups interested in promoting economic growth and social progress.

III. Strategies for Meeting the Challenge

What approaches and measures are developing countries taking to meet this challenge? This question opens up a vast subject covering many different actions and initiatives that have been taken and that are being started every

day. It would be unrealistic to try to give a complete picture. We can,
however, identify some fundamental approaches that have been widely used.

Our discussion will be limited to approaches that represent basic
choices among the main alternatives available, determine the long-term
orientation of a wide range of specific activities, and imply a corresponding
resource allocation. Expressed in other terms, we are going to review
approaches that have a strategic dimension.

Particular strategies have been followed, and these are reviewed and
discussed in some detail here--but they have not always been explicitly stated
or formalized in official documents such as government policy statements or
national development plans. Also, they were not necessarily chosen at any one
time as a complete portfolio. Rather, a pragmatic, muddling-through approach
has prevailed, whereby individual countries have adopted particular approaches
step by step, as they became aware of new needs and estimated that they were
ready to act. This behavior also explains the lack of coordination among
individual strategies and even the existence of conflicting strategies in some
cases.

Certain few strategies, however, were explicitly stated and
officially promoted. In several countries, for example, the replacement of
foreign managerial manpower by local professionals is provided for in laws and
other legal texts that embody a basic strategic choice of government. The
roles of central national institutions in management and administration,
including their relations to public and private organizations, are often
defined by law or government decree. References to the development of
managerial manpower and to targets for the improvement of training and
productivity can be found in national development plans and in the resolutions
of political and technical meetings of national importance. In many

countries, national or sectoral surveys of managerial manpower have been carried out and various action plans based thereon.

However, the national strategy for meeting the management challenge is not approached holistically, as is understandable. Even those political and business leaders who completely understand the management problems of their countries are seldom able to make meaningful recommendations for comprehensive national strategies. This situation reflects the complexity of the problems, the diversity of interests at stake, the availability of alternative approaches among which it is difficult to choose, and the lack of agreement on how roles should be distributed within a national program. Thus, case-by-case, step-by-step, ad hoc approaches prevail.

By and large, the following strategic choices determine how managerial competence and effectiveness is being increased in most developing countries:

- The role assigned to public management,

- The role assigned to private management and entrepreneurship,

- The interaction of public and private management,

- The strategy for localizing management (replacing foreign managerial manpower by nationals),

- The transfer of management expertise from industrialized countries,

- The building of professional institutions and services to management,

- The priority given to the modern economic sectors,

- The role of technical cooperation.

These strategic choices are reviewed below and their interrelationships emphasized. The section concludes with some suggestions for future strategy.

Role Assigned to Public Management

Public management has been assigned a prominent role by developing countries attempting to manage and develop their economies after independence. Since the reasons for this are well known, we need to describe them only briefly.

First, in most developing countries, the political will to stimulate, orient, and accelerate development has spawned new government functions and institutions, which have been made responsible for national planning and coordination, and for defining and putting into effect public policy in areas such as investment, imports, exports, finance, taxation, or regional development. This procedure departs from the traditional approach of colonial administrations interested mainly in maintaining law and order. It has given birth to the concept of development administration, or development management, according to which the primary responsibility of government in a developing country is actively to lead, stimulate, and centrally coordinate the country's total development endeavor.

Second, the decision of governments to manage directly specific economic activities in productive and service sectors was sometimes a consequence of nationalizations, of the departure of foreign owners, of decisions to put up new plants using public money, of decisions to provide new types of public services, and of the fact that private capital and management were often unavailable or unwilling to enter certain areas considered important by the governments. This chain of events generated a large and steadily growing number of public enterprises and agencies in manufacturing, distribution, transport, and other productive and service sectors.

These two major areas--the public management of the development process and the management of individual public enterprises--although closely connected, differ in several respects. As far as public management of a country is concerned, the basic alternative is either to have and implement a national development policy, and to orient and stimulate individual enterprises (both private and public) toward priority goals, or to allow a laissez-faire approach, which has both advantages as well as risks and pitfalls. In the sphere of enterprise management, the basic issue is one of public as against private management of specific organizations. Theoretically, the choice should be guided by economic rationality and priority given to the enterprise that best ensures acceptable service to society for a lower price. In most countries, however, political and ideological criteria and the distribution of power tend to influence the decisions to nationalize and to ban the private sector from certain economic activities.

What, then, have been the main implications of these trends for the development of management capabilities of the Third World countries?

First, the weight of the public sector in the total volume of management activity, hence also in efforts aimed at improving managerial competence and effectiveness, is high in all developing countries. These include mixed economies such as Indonesia, the Ivory Coast, or Venezuela, which have opted for a symbiosis of public and private economy.

Second, the number one priority of all developing countries has been to build a strong public administration of a new type, that is, one able to manage the process of economic and social development. Among the ambitious programs adopted by most governments have been tasks such as establishing new governmental institutions and planning, control, and regulatory systems, or training public personnel for their new functions. These developments took place as an adjustment process, not by destroying, but by restructuring, reforming, and expanding existing public machinery, some of which was inherited from the colonial civil service. Therefore, it was deemed necessary to undertake a vast revision of the structures and practices that were no longer relevant. Comprehensive administrative reforms were designed for this purpose and were gradually implemented with greater or smaller success in most developing countries. To comment on the results of the administrative reforms and assess their real contribution to improving public management in developing countries would exceed the scope of this paper, since few countries have yet evaluated the success of these efforts. It is widely believed that most reform programs had essentially correct objectives and were based on solid analytical and conceptual work, but that most governments lacked energy and resources for bringing the reform programs to a successful end, particularly where difficult and politically sensitive measures were involved (as in the transfer of excess, inefficient personnel to other jobs; the decentralization of public services; or the increase in salaries of underpaid categories of civil servants). Many of these chronic problems in the civil service of developing countries have still not been solved and will have to be addressed by future programs for improving management capabilities.

Third, the linkages between public administrations and public enterprises and the ways in which government exercises control over public enterprises strongly influence both the management of public enterprises and the efforts made to improve their performance. Since public enterprises dominate the modern sector of most of these countries, the effectiveness of their control by government also influences the overall state of the national economy.

It is risky to generalize about public enterprise management, since different enterprises operate under different conditions. Public monopolies provide a single service or product for a government-controlled price, whereas some other enterprises compete with the private sector in domestic and international markets. Some public concerns are well-established and have managerial know-how and a strong tradition inherited from the private sector (for example, some national oil and mining corporations), whereas others are very young and inexperienced. Then, too, some enterprises were created in response to a well-defined need, whereas others exist "by accident" (some plants, for example, were acquired and put up without a feasibility study, while some units were nationalized in a particular political atmosphere with no economic or other justification for being placed in the public sector). These different conditions must be kept in mind in examining the alternative strategies for improving managerial competence and evaluating the results of public enterprises. These tasks should be easier in enterprises fully exposed to strong external economic forces, such as the market test. They may be impossible in enterprises that may have been created in error and that could not exist without large, permanent government subsidies.

In all public enterprises, however, the management standards achieved and the approaches used to improve management performance reflect their dependence on government administration and the ways in which the government treats its enterprises. Almost all Third World countries regard and treat their public enterprises not as enterprises, but as another arm of the public service, even though many enterprises must sell their produce for competitive prices. In other words, the adjective "public" is given more weight than the

substantive "enterprise." As a result of that fundamental attitude, the door
has been opened to an endless range of bureaucratic interventions in the
operations of these enterprises—including interventions that create
additional costs (political appointments or measures forcing the enterprise to
employ excess manpower) and prevent the enterprise from using normal
managerial measures (such as adjusting salary structures to the labor market
situation), but that also help it to survive relatively easily despite
substandard performance. Governments are reluctant to increase the autonomy
of public enterprises, relax the very detailed controls, and require full
responsibility of management teams. All the economic and social consequences
of this bureaucratic conception of the management of public enterprises are
yet to be evaluated; however, such an evaluation is likely to show that this
conception has been responsible for considerable damage to the fragile
economies of many developing countries and for the slow development of
appropriate managerial competence within the public sector.

The approaches to management development and performance improvement
have to be seen against this complex background. The two principal approaches
being used at present are the "training approach" and the "consulting
approach." The training approach regards inadequate training as the main
cause of low performance; hence more training is given to personnel at all
levels (including those in central and local government who are involved in
controlling public enterprises). It is assumed that well-trained managers
will perform better and thus overall organizational performance will start
improving. The consulting approach, which is favored by many governments and
aid agencies, relies on experienced (sometimes even the best in the world)
consultants to diagnose the enterprise in depth. Excellent reports are
normally produced, including long lists of practical recommendations. A third

approach is sometimes used that combines the previous two. In these cases, the government might review an enterprise and issue instructions to its top management, as well as various government departments concerned, about what to change; in addition, managers are sent to courses. This third approach, coming from the top, could be called a "ministerial approach."

The results of these approaches tend to be disappointing in that: (1) because the managers and other employees within the organizations are not involved, they become passive rather than motivated and responsible for the success of a performance improvement program; and (2) training seems to have no connection with the identification and solution of real priority problems, and there seems to be no link between internal and external forces influencing an organization in achieving its objectives.

The experience of a number of ILO projects assisting public enterprises confirms that the most feasible and promising current approach is one that does not tackle all problems of a particular public enterprise (or a group of enterprises) at once, since the task may really be too big and the existing obstacles insurmountable. These projects have found that at least 60 percent, and in some cases more than 75 percent of problems identified by enterprise managers have been within the latter's competence. The task is to motivate the managers to act. Also, it appears that many external and environmental problems can be tackled more easily if an enterprise demonstrates that it has started a performance improvement program, but cannot continue unless its ministry changes a regulation, accelerates the approval procedure for import licences, pays the public enterprises correctly for the services supplied, and so on. Constructive pressure and specific proposals coming from many enterprises will have a much greater impact than a general suggestion coming from some high-level committee handling the same issue. If action from the bottom can be harmonised with action from the top at some stage in the process, the changes of success will be greater.

Role Assigned to Private Management and Entrepreneurship

The history of management is linked to the history of the private business corporation in Europe and North America, and more recently in Japan. Most innovations in management techniques and systems, including those widely used in the public sector, originated in private management. The role of the private sector in building the managerial capabilities of developing countries is therefore another strategic dimension and has to be seen in a historical perspective. 2/

The initial attitudes toward private business and management reflected the political forces let loose by the decolonization process. Many nationalizations were judged politically necessary, while in other countries no private enterprises, local or foreign, were interested in projects that the governments decided to launch. In some countries the official attitude toward the private sector was motivated by ideology: private enterprise was regarded as unsuitable for a developing economy and the profit motive was viewed as suspect, since it could not guarantee a growing supply of the most needed products and services. Private management was therefore excluded from the more important and prospective economic activities. A few governments even preferred to tolerate a chronic shortage of consumer goods, deficient services, and a flourishing black market rather than officially authorize and encourage private industrial initiative.

At present, an increasingly pragmatic attitude toward private management is evolving in the developing countries, even among regimes that were originally hostile toward any private business, but that have been able to learn from their own economic experience and that of their neighbors. This experience has shown that the development process requires a massive mobilization of human energy, initiative, and creativity on one side, and of material and financial resources controlled by individuals or groups of persons on the other. More and more countries have recognized that resources that can be mobilized through the public savings and public borrowing are inadequate to meet the needs of the developing countries, and that private savings and private initiative must play a growing role in the developing world. Even developing countries that have not favored a market economy and that have relied on central planning are concluding that many goods will never be available on the market, many services will never be provided, and the bulk of private savings will never be mobilized for development if indigenous entrepreneurs are not encouraged to create new enterprises and apply personal talent and drive to their growth.

Pragmatism avoids a priori definitions of the respective roles of the public, private, and mixed enterprises. Instead of viewing these sectors as antagonistic and mutually exclusive, pragmatic policymakers try to analyze which type of enterprise is likely to manage and perform better in each case, and they bear in mind both the criteria of economic rationality and efficiency as well as the broad national goals and interests. Where appropriate, this pragmatic approach encourages direct competition between public and private enterprises in serving the same market.

Certain people play a critical role in starting new private enterprises: the entrepreneurs. They are keen to start and succeed in business without waiting for instructions or pushes from an administrative or other authority. They are able to detect and evaluate opportunities and to take advantage of them. Their characteristics include personal drive, self-confidence, originality, task-result orientation, willingness to take calculated risks, and the ability to provide leadership. All these qualities are badly needed in the developing world. Abraham Maslow, the American psychologist, once said that if requested to help a country in distress, he would send them neither 100 soldiers nor 100 teachers, but 100 entrepreneurs. It would be difficult to summarize the social function of entrepreneurship in a better way. History demonstrates this function in countries that have reached the highest levels in industrial development and GNP per capita. Current experience is demonstrating this function in the middle-income group of developing countries, which have been able to create and develop many new industries using primarily their own resources, or to combine local talent with talent and resources provided by other countries.

The traditional cultures and social structures of some developing countries inhibit available entrepreneurial talent. Thus, the limited opportunities that existed in the past--for example, in wholesale and retail trade--were taken up by foreign minorities, such as the Lebanese in Western Africa, the Indians in Eastern Africa, or the Chinese in Southeast Asia. The shortage of indigenous entrepreneurs has historical causes. Economic development is not possible unless that shortage can be overcome.

Almost all developing countries are now committed to promoting entrepreneurship, although some of them assign only a restricted role to the indigenous private sector and some others have not really started putting their intentions into effect. Public policy and regulatory functions are essential, as they constitute an environment that can encourage or discourage local entrepreneurial initiative. The political situation is equally important, as it has to create an atmosphere of stability, confidence, and social encouragement, without which economic incentives do not work. In several African countries, for example, private entrepreneurs live in uncertainty, afraid of expropriation and of excessive government control and interference.

Debate continues on the strategies needed to directly assist and promote the small enterprise. Some argue that if the environment is not adverse to entrepreneurship, the small businessman "will take care of himself," as has has been the case in Singapore and South Korea, where entrepreneurial initiative has helped to accelerate industrialization. The elaborate systems used in some countries--whereby small businessmen are sought, identified, trained, helped to launch a business, and then "nursed" by a government agency--are more and more considered to be too cumbersome and not very successful. Some interesting experiences are discussed in Part III of the paper.

Thus far, no satisfying solutions have been found for least developed countries with no entrepreneurial tradition and limited sources of indigenous entrepreneurial talent. The lack of entrepreneurial tradition and experience is reflected in local culture: entrepreneurship may be less respectable than other careers and the development of entrepreneurial attitudes and behaviors is not sufficiently encouraged by the social environment, whether it be the family, school, or community. Young people have little opportunity to acquire entrepreneurial skills under these circumstances.

Education at home and at school can play a critical role in creating a value system that encourages entrepreneurship, initiative, and creativity. This has been the case in some countries with an impressive record of achievement in industrial and business development. But even the United States--where economic wealth has been built on private entrepreneurship par excellence--is witnessing an erosion of values favoring entrepreneurship and business initiative. The National Business Education Association recently recommended that basic business education should be revitalized at all instructional levels. 3/ Above all, it argued, the American school system can and should be more effective in preparing youth for future business activity.

Although a least developed country could not copy this example, it can seek inspiration in it. The general and technical education and the vocational training systems in developing countries can help tremendously in molding positive attitudes toward entrepreneurship and in providing young people with an elementary knowledge of economics and a range of basic numerical, organizational, commercial, and other skills needed in business. This is a most neglected area, one to which future strategies should pay particular attention and in which action is overdue.

As for the medium-size and larger local private enterprises in developing countries, their role in building national managerial capabilities has increased considerably over the last decade in the middle-income countries, which have adopted an accelerated industrialization strategy and opted for a mixed economy. This role has been more limited in the least developed countries, but even there, some indigenous private enterprises have grown rapidly and have made a concerted effort to install an appropriate management system and train their personnel.

The pressure of the market and the will to be competitive have clearly influenced the drive for managerial effectiveness among companies. This has been the case in countries such as Brazil, India, Morocco, the Philippines, Singapore, and South Korea, particularly among their exporting industries and enterprises that have to compete with imported goods. In general, they were able to offer higher salaries to managerial and technical personnel and thus attract competent accountants, marketing specialists, and plant managers, including some previously employed by public enterprises.

However, many interesting developments in the management of dynamic private firms of developing countries are not sufficiently known. They should be studied and their experience made known to firms and countries that follow a similar path.

The local subsidiaries of multinational corporations have also played a role in the management scene. In a developing country this scene is influenced by the corporations' share in local busness activity and by the choice of sectors in which they operate. Management experience of the whole corporation is available to its local subsidiary and the standards applied there tend to be higher than in other local enterprises, private and public. The corporations' interregional and regional training programs are used extensively by their subsidiaries; in many cases local managerial staff are trained and retrained in accordance with a multinational company's worldwide scheme. 4/

There are also problems, however. The higher salaries offered to managerial personnel tend to attract trained staff from the government and local businesses, for example, whereas the opposite seldom occurs. In some cases, only a limited range of technical and managerial functions has been decentralized to a local subsidiary, or only lower and middle-level managerial positions have been localized. When it comes to particular functions, international companies tend to prefer centralized financial and personnel policy and research. The location of research facilities and the management of research are particularly delicate subjects, about which the host country and the international company often disagree.

Opportunities for making the management experience of a well-established multinational firm available to young local firms--for example, through subcontracting supplemented by training, assistance to local training

programs, or advice to management--could be used to a greater extent.
International companies desire to be perceived as good citizens, whose
presence is not merely tolerated but viewed as an integral part of national
development. Their enthusiasm in this respect creates new opportunities for
using their tremendous management know-how for the wider benefit of the host
countries.

Interaction of Public and Private Management

Most developing countries have mixed economies in which the public
and private sectors have their specific problems and approaches to improving
managerial competence and performance. Since they coexist in one cultural,
political, and economic system, however, they also share certain needs and
opportunities. Their "common denominator" is often overlooked and the
"unique" conditions and objectives of each sector are overstressed. Many have
argued, for example, that public managers and private managers, in developing
countries should not be trained together. Experience shows, however, that
public and private managers should be encouraged to know each other better, to
learn from each other, and to build cooperation links between the two
sectors. In the public sector of many developing countries, the absence of
entrepreneurial and managerial attitudes and the predominance of traditional
civil service attitudes hamper development. Why not promote training and
cooperation programs that expose public managers to the attitudes and work
methods of their private sector peers? Curiously enough, such programs are
common in industrialized countries but are regarded with suspicion in many
developing countries.

In general, it would appear that closer interaction and cooperation
of public and private management could accelerate the upgrading of a country's
total management competence. For example, many governments operate extensive

and costly public services (such as public works departments, suburban transport, waste disposal, or cleaning of cities) and face tremendous problems in managing these services effectively. In some developing countries, such services have been contracted to private firms. This can be done in various ways, for example, through direct contracts or by issuing licences to private firms for providing a defined range of services on approved terms. Public management intervention is limited to policy and control. Such arrangements may require a revision of government procedures to enable individual small contractors, or groups of contractors, to offer their services to the government and submit tenders for jobs exceeding the potential of a single local firm.

Mixed enterprises and joint ventures are a fairly well-known form of cooperation between the public and private sectors, a form that is expanding rapidly and which has a generally positive impact on the quality of enterprise management. Some of the successful enterprises in developing countries in all regions have been founded, financed, and managed by the local public sector in cooperation with private business—local, foreign, or both. These enterprises have benefited not only from the technological and commercial know-how of their private partners, but also from their managerial culture and expertise. Linking a developing country's public enterprise with a multinational corporation in a joint venture often helps to change some of the public sector management practices that were holding back the further development of a public enterprise. 5/

The experience of Japan illustrates how government and public management can facilitate and stimulate the growth of a country's private industrial sector. Its Ministry of International Trade and Industry (MITI) has played a prominent role in promoting technological change, high-quality products, productivity improvement, and exports to industrialized countries.

Strategy for Localizing Management

A decision to localize (indigenize, Africanize, and so on) management is an expression of national sovereignty in an area considered to be critical for the country's future. Such a decision always has a political dimension and, in some countries, the political pressure clearly prevailed after independence in decisions about the extent to which foreigners would be replaced with local people and the time that would be involved. This strategy affected management in both the public and private sectors, although it was not necessarily applied in the same way in both sectors. As a rule, things moved faster in public administration and public enterprises than in the private sector.

Some countries accelerated localization immediately after independence. Other countries--for example, Nigeria, Malaysia, or Indonesia-- introduced programs of successive localization, using ratios of indigenous to foreign personnel, financial incentives encouraging the recruitment of nationals, special permit schemes, and the like. In Indonesia, expatriate work permits are renewed annually and companies have to justify their wish to continue to employ a foreign manager or technician. Larger organizations have to submit localization plans to government authorities.

A third group of countries declared localization to be a long-term objective, but without putting too much pressure on businesses to implement it rapidly. This group includes countries open to foreign investors, some whose "bargaining position" with foreign corporations is weak, as well as special cases of oil-producing and other countries with acute shortages of skilled managers and technicians. In some African countries, for example, localization still has a long way to go. In the Central African Republic, 63 percent of the managers and higher level technicians in the industrial sector in 1980 were foreigners, while in Zambia in 1977, 69 percent of general managers and 81 percent of work managers were expatriates. In the Republic of Cameroon, a 1982 survey showed that while 88 percent of higher level positions were localized in public enterprises, the figure for private, foreign-owned enterprises was 31.6 percent, and for the larger construction and public works establishments only 8 percent. In the Saudi Arabian Aramco, operating in a different context, the number of Americans employed increased from 8.25 percent in 1975 to 9.90 percent in 1980, while over the same period the number of all foreign employees increased from 23.6 percent to 46.4 percent of the staff. 6/ Forecasts indicate that, in eight labor-importing Arab countries, industrialization will require them to employ 72.2 percent expatriates in high-level professional and technical positions in 1985, while the share of expatriates in total manpower requirements will be only 35.1 percent. 7/

A recent survey of attitudes and management practices of 129 international companies 8/ provides insight into the personnel policies of their foreign subsidiaries. Although multinational corporations respect the policies of governments, they often want to negotiate specific practices. The principal reasons for localizing management are: (1) local nationals are absolutely necessary for doing business in certain environments (mainly because of strict government regulations or other pressures); (2) local professionals usually understand the local culture and environment better; (3) employing local nationals often helps to improve morale in local operations; and (4) it is increasingly difficult to find competent nationals from industrialized countries who will accept long-term foreign assignments. Eighty percent of U.S. companies abroad and 70 percent of their European counterparts employ local nationals at the head of most of these operations. But very few international companies would use nationals from developing countries as top managers or board members at headquarters. Different industries hold different views on localizing management. Companies making and selling products in the same country (for example, Unilever) have gone further in localizing the management of their subsidiaries than companies in high-technology fields, whose products have to be exported and continuously updated and which are affected by international inflation.

It could be argued that, in developed countries, the trend is toward integration and a relatively free transfer of high-level technical and managerial personnel from country to country, and that a rigid localization policy can be counterproductive and should only be temporary. Here a mechanistic comparison between industrialized and developing countries can be misleading. In the developed countries, frequent transfers of high-level personnel occur in a quite different economic and social context. In developing countries, a purposeful and perserverant localization policy is a must: without it, the more complex and difficult managerial functions might remain in foreign hands too long.

Localization policy means more, however, than merely replacing people of one nationality with those of another. It means preparing the new managers for future responsibilities, through education, selection, induction, training, career planning, and on-the-job guidance.

Learning on the job, historically the first "method" used to develop managers in industrialized countries, is the principal method even today. It is now commonly supplemented and accelerated by management education and training, and managers can also turn to a wide range of consulting and other professional services. In developing countries, the learning-by-doing

approach was first adopted not so much deliberately, but as a necessity
following the political choice concerning localization of management, the
departure of expatriate managers, and the rapid creation of numerous new
managerial jobs in the public and private sectors.

Under the circumstances, governments and local businesses started
filling vacant managerial positions with individuals of varying educational
backgrounds, but mostly with people lacking management experience. Since most
of these managers were new in their positions, few enjoyed the benefits of
learning from more experienced superiors and peers. They learned by trial and
error, from foreign advisers, by attending programs of accelerated training,
through study tours, and so on. Young university graduates also had to learn
management primarily on the job, since few were educated in management and
administration. Real managerial talents were quickly able to demonstrate
their abilities: these are the people who, at present, constitute the core of
the new managerial class in the developing countries.

Those most recently entering managerial jobs tend to be better
trained for management and can already learn from the first generation of
"pioneers." They will be receiving better support from their chiefs and also
from professional institutions. But learning on the job will continue to be
the main method of acquiring management skills and attaining high levels of
professional excellence.

Many organizations have benefited less from on-the-job learning
because they have failed to use the experience of foreign managers in training
their indigenous successors. Of those who had to leave following government
policy decisions, few were very keen to pass on their experience, and many had
to leave their jobs before a successor was found.

Even now, certain practices adversely affect on-the-job learning. The transfer of experience is constrained by excessively high staff turnover; haphazard transfers and appointments (called conveyor-belt management) that do not use accumulated experience; the growing brain drain in some countries; and the reluctance of senior managers to delegate and decentralize, and thus accelerate, the learning of the middle and junior managers.

Transfer of Management Expertise from Industrialized Countries

Since independence, the developing countries have relied on the transfer of management and administration techniques and systems from industrialized countries as an important strategy in both the private and public sectors. Without local management traditions, or sufficient capability to quickly develop and apply original management systems reflecting each country's needs and conditions, transfer seemed the only alternative.

Five main transfer channels have been used:

(1) Already existing systems (inherited from the pre-independence era) were largely maintained to ensure continuity and stability.

(2) New systems were acquired ad hoc in the framework of investment projects (the suppliers of a new plant provided a management system and some training with the contract).

(3) Multinational corporations often brought with them their enterprise management systems.

(4) The engineers, economists, and administrators trained abroad returned home with a knowledge of particular foreign systems, which they applied in their new jobs.

(5) Technical assistance projects and the use of foreign consultants in administration, management, sectoral development, export promotion, and so on was an important vehicle for transferring foreign management systems.

The total "package" of management techniques and systems transferred differs from country to country. Administrative systems, for example, have been strongly influenced not only by the pre-independence tradition, but also by continued links with former colonial powers. These ties remained after independence and often were strengthened again after a period of cooling down in the first post-independence years. Some countries—for example, those in Latin America—have turned increasingly to North American administrative experience. In enterprise management, techniques and systems from North America have generally prevailed, even though some of them did not reach the developing countries directly, but through Europe, and with certain modifications. In the new functions of government, such as national planning, or directing and controlling the public enterprises, the transfer of management systems tended to follow the countries' principal developmental and political options: while the majority was interested primarily in Western European approaches, some developing countries sought experience from Eastern Europe.

During the past ten years, a different strategy was repeatedly called for by the developing countries themselves, by international agencies, and by many scholars of social sciences, all of whom argued that the methods could not be transferred without adaptation to local conditions and that priority had to be given to original, locally developed and tested techniques and systems. In particular, it was suggested the decision on what management system or technique to promote should be based on the specific human, cultural, and social conditions of the country and on deeply rooted behavioral patterns.

This strategy, however, is a most difficult one to carry out. As far back as 1965, the ILO undertook a study of social and cultural factors in management development in a number of countries. Results were reviewed by experts and widely disseminated. 9/ Seventeen years later, another study, based on recent research, addressed similar questions. 10/ Not surprisingly, both studies identified the same cultural problems and noted that it was difficult to apply foreign management techniques and systems in developing societies. Although it would be unrealistic to expect a drastic change over such a short time, it is equally alarming to find that the progress has been so modest and that, in most developing countries, so little is being done to resolve the conflict between modern management concepts and traditional social structures and cultures.

Some management techniques were originally developed in response to particular technical characteristics of organizations, such as the nature and complexity of the technology used, or the amount of data to be recorded and analyzed within particular time limits. Such techniques are concerned primarily with the technological, economic, and financial side of organizations, and thus are relatively neutral and should fit different cultures. However, the application of a technique, no matter how neutral and universal, creates a new work situation that may conflict with personal interests, values, and habits. A production control or maintenance management technique required by the technology used may conflict with a worker's beliefs and habits concerning punctuality, work discipline, justified absence from work, accuracy and reliability of records, and the like.

Techniques and systems used in managing the human side of organizations relate directly to cultural and social values. Many of these techniques are difficult to transfer, or their transfer may even cause adverse effects. For example, remuneration plans that stimulate individual performance, rather than collective solidarity and performance are not well received in collectivist societies; organization development methods using confrontation techniques cannot succeed where harmony and the avoidance of conflict are highly valued; problem-solving approaches built on democratic values are difficult to apply in autocratic cultures; and matrix organization does not work well in cultures in which the people prefer unity of command and orders from a single higher authority.

Multinational corporations operating in developing countries face specific cultural problems in managing their subsidiaries and co-managing joint-venture companies. One problem is that they have to bring with them their own organizational cultures in order to maintain identity and homogeneity of operations in dozens of countries. 11/ As a rule, this organizational culture, strongly influenced by the national culture of the corporation's home country, produces a special cultural mix in local subsidiaries. Multinational corporations follow different strategies; some emphasise their organizational culture and seek local managers who are able to understand and adopt it. They regard this approach to be essential in maintaining communication and a productive relationship with the headquarters. Others prefer a "low-profile" presence, deemphasizing their own organizational values, habits, and procedures, and adapting as much as possible to "local ways of perceiving and doing business."

Culture, however, is not static, and does not operate as a social sieve through which certain management methods pass and others do not. European history provides ample evidence of dramatic social and cultural changes engendered by industrialization and new technology. Culture and social structures change and will continue to change in the developing world under the influence of changes in conditions of living, nutrition, education, communications, technology, and industrialization.

To better match management systems to local conditions, a special effort will be required in the developing countries themselves, for example, in their enterprises, government departments, educational and training institutions, and social organizations. The best talents and brains have to be mobilized for this task. Various sectors require different approaches: it is in the traditional sectors that foreign management systems usually fail. There, the need for innovative ways of managing and administrating the development process and local services to the population is most pressing.

A new strategy will require, among other considerations, considerable strengthening of management and administrative research in developing countries. 12/ In particular, this research must not only identify the sociocultural factors that will explain why certain approaches transplanted from abroad do not produce the expected results, but must also identify methods and systems that have been developed, or adapted, and then used successfully in local practice. The experience of organizations and countries must be compared and promising experience generalized and disseminated. The results of research into new local methods and systems should be relfected in the curricula of management education and training.

Building of Professional Institutions and Services to Management

On-the-job learning is slow and risky. A manager who learns only on the job may never learn about the management experience of other organizations and countries. Management education, training, and consulting and various information sources, publications, and training materials are therefore needed to ensure that such experience and guidance will reach a particular manager who wants to know more than he can learn within his own organization and its immediate environment. This form of education and development also includes screening and evaluating generalized experience and extracting from it what appears most relevant to a particular job. To respond to this need, many developing countries established national professional institutions and services for management, and used them not only to accelerate the training and development of managerial manpower, but also to solve various practical management and administrative problems.

Most industrialized countries have used this strategy, too. In Western Europe, for example, several national productivity agencies and centers were established after World War II followed in the 1950s and 1960s by the creation of new management faculties, schools, and centers in all European countries. In the United States, the network of schools of business administration that already existed before World War II expanded vigorously and diversified their services after 1945. After all, almost all management institutions in industrialized countries are still new. In following this worldwide trend, the developing countries created their national management institutions at a much earlier stage of industrial and economic development than did the industrialized countries.

This institution-building strategy has led to the establishment of an impressive number of management institutes, schools, and centers throughout the developing world. Although the smaller and poorer countries have established only a few such centers, larger countries with more diversified economies (such as Brazil, India, or Nigeria), have dozens of institutions, the specialization and mandates of which have been defined in many different ways. 13/ Many types can be found: there are productivity and management training centers and institutes, staff colleges, management and business schools, schools and institutions of administration, as well as institutions specialized sectorally (for example, construction, transportation, small business) or functionally (financial management, accountancy training, marketing, computer training, and so on). They represent a considerable investment in high-level manpower and facilities and their intellectual potential is tremendous. In addition, new institutions continue to be created, while many existing institutions need strengthening and require further support in order to provide the full range of services for which they were established. It is therefore most appropriate to ask whether their potential is sufficiently utilized and, if not, what to do to utilize it more effectively.

Some existing institutions do not respond to real needs, but they are rare. But the issue is one of design and management. An institution's potential for playing a significant social role is not questioned, but perhaps the approach originally taken in designing the institution and starting its first programs has not been fully adapted to the given developmental context. Or perhaps the accumulation of human, financial, administrative, and other difficulties in planning and developing the institution have caused it to fall short of expectations.

Some countries suffer from a proliferation and fragmentation of institutions. Despite extreme shortages of professional manpower and finance, various ministries and central bodies prefer to have their own institutions rather than to share one large enough and equipped enough to generate a critical mass of professional competence. Often the initial feasibility study underestimated the recurrent cost of running an institution, which may be dangerously high even if the buildings were donated and a team of foreign experts acting as a "free resource" initially helped the institution.

As already mentioned, in developing countries, most institutional activities for improving management and training and educating managerial manpower are government-initiated, government-sponsored, and government-administered. Consequently, most management institutions, including those established for the local private sector, are public sector institutions. This has helped to mobilize resources and emphasize the importance of a new institution. The great drawback is that institutions suffer from the very same ills that they should be helping to cure in client organizations--they are designed and operated as public bureaucracies, even though their principal objective is to develop businesslike and entrepreneurial attitudes and skills. Striped animals raise spotted ones with difficulty. A few institutions were given considerable autonomy and were modeled on a well-organized and dynamic enterprise rather than on a public service unit. However, most management institutions are governed by public personnel, financial, and administrative regulations developed for government departments. Their operating autonomy is limited. This situation affects their staffing as well as the remuneration of personnel, work methods, and value systems. Few feel responsible for progressive changes in the client system, that is, in the enterprises or government agencies for whose benefit they were established. Too few developing countries have private and independent management institutions established, for example, by groups of private businesses or by management associations. Their number and impact are negligible.

The influence of both private and public enterprises on the orientation and operation of management institutes and centers is not as great as influence of government departments to which these institutions report. Even if some public and private sector managers are members of institution boards, few in managerial circles regard the management institutions as organizations that they own and for which they are co-responsible. This situation has created a vicious circle that is difficult to break.

Institutions are criticized for being too academic, for pursuing their own objectives rather than those of local businesses, and for being only marginally useful to the practitioners. The practicioners who make these statements, however, do not understand that management institutions also reflect the concerns and values of local businesses and that no authority can make institutions more relevant and effective if business does not clearly define its requirements, does not care about institutions, and does not offer help to them.

Some management institutions were located at universities, with the mandate to educate and train new generations of managers and administrators through undergraduate or graduate programs. Their principal problem has been the paralyzing influence of the conservative university environment, which overrates academic goals and criteria and underrates the needs of the world of practice. Consequently, many curricula of management studies replicate models provided by very advanced industrial countries and turn out graduates ill-prepared to face practical situations of local enterprises.

Staffing is another serious problem affecting the capacity and credibility of management institutions. Many institutions were first staffed by teachers and trainers who had no practical experience. Personnel problems were exacerbated by low salaries and a high turnover of staff. This situation has improved, thanks to training and experience acquired on the job, but too few institutions have a professional staff that can be asked to deal with important practical problems. Similar difficulties are faced by many indigenous consulting and accounting firms established by young and relatively inexperienced management professionals. 14/

A typical service portfolio of management institutions includes training and educational activities, consulting and advisory activities, and research and information services. Invariably, the main focus has been on training. Both in enterprise management and public administration, the new institutions became responsible for training large numbers of national staff in a wide range of courses and seminars, supplementing on-the-job learning, and even replacing it if inexperienced staff had to be quickly prepared for new functions. The total training effort of management institutions is impossible to measure and evaluate accurately, but it has been enormous in all the developing countries. Its main contribution has been to build up the knowledge of management and administrative methods and techniques. Substantial improvements in trainee skills have been achieved only by those institutions that were able to link institutional training to in-plant and on-the-job training and that helped managers attending courses solve meaningful practical problems.

These results suggest that the portfolio of institutional services must be seen and managed as a whole, in which the elements complement and support each other. In a developing country, moreover, this portfolio should provide skills and help make changes in important areas where the government, as well as private and public enterprises, are keen to make improvements. Wherever management institutions are not closely linked to the world of practice, their effectiveness and credibility are low.

An effort worthy of note was undertaken by a group of management institutions in Asia and Latin America, working and exchanging experience in the management of social development. Their experience has been described and summarized in a model called the "learning-intervening process," 15/ which has the following features. Management research in institutions is problem-centered rather than theory-building and includes direct work with managers, not just with other researchers, to test the validity and usefulness of their

tentative research conclusions. These conclusions are brought back to the
classroom as locally relevant teaching materials. Through their consulting,
they try to increase the problem-solving capabilities of the managers rather
than just to solve their problems for them. Consulting and training both aim
to improve organization structures and management systems, not just to build
up the skills of individuals. Seminars bring together key people from a
single organization on programs to instill spirit and build skills. Seminars
are designed to produce behavioral changes identified as important during
diagnostic studies of the client.

Drawing lessons from a number of management development projects
implemented over the last thirty years, the ILO Management Development
Programme has identified several characteristics of an "effective management
development institution." They have not been summarized in the form of a
model mainly because of the great variety of situations in which institutions
operate and also the varying expectations of their constituents. It is
difficult to say that, to be effective, an institution must possess all the
characteristics included in a general model. Instead of undertaking its own
research, for example, it could collaborate with other institutions and use
the results of their research activity. Nonetheless, it is possible to
indicate tendencies and to describe the characteristics of institutional set-
ups and behaviors that tend to contribute to success in most cases. [16]

Effective management institutions in developing countries exhibit the
following eleven characteristics:

(1)   The client base is clearly defined (it is homogenous if
        possible) and the institution is very closely linked to it.

(2)   The institution is pro-active; that is, it considers itself
        socially co-responsible for the state of management and

administration in its country and readily takes the initiative
in proposing and implementing improvement measures.

(3)   The institution has a strong practical bias; that is, it views
practical improvements in management and administration as the
ultimate goal (even if the main activity is teaching or
research).

(4)   It practises strategic management in defining its purpose,
objectives, and portfolio of services; in allocating and
developing resources; and in harmonizing the various choices
made.

(5)   It uses a properly selected and coherent portfolio of
intervention methods (training, teaching, consulting, various
types of research collection and dissemination of information,
social work, and so on) in serving the client base, learning
from it, and linking teaching and training with the
identification and solving of practical problems.

(6)   Its approach is interdisciplinary and problem oriented rather
than discipline oriented.

(7)   The staff is regarded as the institution's most precious
resource; its professional integrity, motivation and competence
are high, and its profile coherent with the institution's
strategic choices and intervention methods; the staff has both
a strong theoretical background and a solid practical bias;
staff turnover is low.

(8)   Leadership is considered to be critically important: the
institution's head is accepted and acts as a true leader, both

within and outside the institution, and stays in his position
for a sufficiently long time.

(9)   The institution is run as a flexible and efficient enterprise
rather than as an administrative unit of government; its
operational management makes sure that strategies and plans are
implemented and the cost of services kept to the necessary
minimum.

(10)   It enjoys considerable autonomy, but is accountable to its
constituents for performance results.

(11)   Evaluation at all levels is practised on a regular basis;
periodic self-appraisal is used to assess performance, adjust
strategy to new opportunities, and improve what needs to be
improved under items (1)-(10)

All in all, we are currently witnessing some disenchantment with
institution building in management and administration. Institutions
everywhere are being criticized, and even their positive achievements and
experiences are being belittled. There is a need to agree on a new strategy
aimed at restructuring institutions, streamlining their national networks in
some cases, reinforcing their linkages with the client base, enlisting the
support of local business, enhancing autonomy and responsibility for results,
and increasing the role of institutions in developing local management
patterns. Some promising experiences are reviewed in Part III.

Priority Given to the Modern Economic Sector

The development strategy pursued by the developing countries in the
first post-independence period emphasized the modern economic sector. This
included manufacturing, petroleum and gas, mining, the generation and
distribution of power, communications, and modern agriculture. Public

administration and the military also belong to the modern sector in the broad sense of the term. This approach has dichotomized developing societies and created dual economies, as already mentioned at the outset. The implications for management have been far reaching.

Although the modern sector may be a small part of the total economic activity of a country, it demands the most managerial manpower and attract most human talents and the bulk of financial resources available for building management structures and capabilities. It generally offers more interesting careers, salaries, and conditions of living than other sectors. As a result, the scarce technical and managerial manpower tends to concentrate in the modern sector. These conditions affect the profile of management institutions, which have been built primarily to serve the modern sector-- manufacturing and some other industries and services, as well as central government administration. Management institutions are therefore part of the modern sector, and their value system and institutional and personal objectives are tied to the further growth and development of this sector. Multinational corporations, joint ventures, and various forms of technological and economic cooperation with foreign firms also contribute to the strengthening of management in the modern sector.

The so-called "social" (or "social development") sectors include traditional agriculture and handicrafts, rural and community development, basic education, literacy programs, food distribution, and health and population control. At present, these sectors are being assigned increasing priority in the national development strategies of many countries. However, policy decisions and even considerable resource allocations alone cannot quickly and dramatically change the management scene.

Social development programs and organizations are managed differently from a manufacturing plant or a department of the central government. Their managers do not control well-determined and structured production and administrative processes, but aim to improve living conditions and productivity in traditional rural communities and among the urban poor. Since the rural and urban poor constitute the main "clientele" of these programs, the managerial work is more psychological, social, and cultural in nature than technological. A manager must be versatile, enterprising, and able to find imaginative and unorthodox solutions, using limited resources in conditions of imperfection. He must be prepared to cope with difficult living conditions and accept less remuneration than his colleagues in industry. Unfortunately, higher education, both at home and overseas in industrialized countries, seldom prepares graduates for organizational and managerial work in social development programs.

The problems are exacerbated by the virtual impossibility of finding relevant expertise for managing rural and social development in industrialized countries. Developing countries are tackling virgin ground in this field, and must rely almost entirely on their own imagination, creativity, and experience.

The dichotomy of the modern and social sectors is a formidable management challenge. One must emphasize the interdependence of the two sectors, and note that the growth of the modern sector will stop unless the vast traditional economy and social structures change. This means the development of managerial capabilities and effectiveness as well. Poor management of social development and services and considerable sectoral discrepancies in the standards of management already adversely affect the performance of the modern sector, which does not exist in a vacuum but is connected to the traditional sectors through many economic, social, and cultural links.

Because of their specific skill requirements and other conditions, the social sectors must find managerial talent mainly from within, that is, among committed, able people who have been involved in social development. However, this alone does not suffice. Public and private enterprises, government agencies, universities, and management institutions of the modern sector must also contribute to social development and accept specific responsibilities in helping the social sectors to build their management competence. 17/

Role of Technical Cooperation

Technical cooperation has played a major role in building up the management capabilities and institutions of developing countries. All developing countries rely on it for acquiring on the experience of industrialized countries. They also use it to supplement limited local professional manpower and to obtain financial support for projects that otherwise would be beyond their reach.

It is important to grasp the real nature and the strategic implications of technical cooperation in this area. Most projects involving teams of foreign advisers and trainers were planned and carried out when the receiving countries were searching for appropriate development strategies and were structuring and building up their policymaking bodies. Technical cooperation projects were therefore involved not only in strategy implementation, but also in making fundamental strategic decisions about management and administration issues. Despite their essentially advisory role, their influence on decisions was strong. Choosing a particular donor country and agency (if there was a choice) usually meant choosing particular country models and the range of expertise from which the receiving country could draw. As a result, the donors and organizers of technical assistance are co-responsible for the strategies pursued by the developing countries.

Certain differences between bilateral and multilateral assistance ought to be mentioned. Bilateral assistance is used mainly to transfer the expertise of the donor country. It is tied to certain ideas, approaches, technologies, and institutions. Since many bilateral projects are concerned with national development planning, with monetary, fiscal, and investment policy, and with related national legislation, and are attached to central policymaking bodies, they forge close relationships between the donor and the recipient on important national issues, and tend to transfer the donor's own model, or to reinforce this model wherever assistance is provided by donor countries to their former colonies.

In multilateral assistance, the donor and executing agencies aim at choosing from the best experience available internationally. They try to take an objective and balanced approach, for example, by fielding multinational teams, organizing study tours to several countries, or preparing training materials based on international experience. Language and other barriers, of course, are difficult to overcome.

Some other lessons from technical assistance in management and administration are worth mentioning. First, the administrative and managerial weaknesses of the developing countries are reflected in the way they program and coordinate technical assistance. Individual ministries, institutions, and even enterprises try to capture their own projects and expert teams, often ignoring what is already available in other projects. They may cooperate with several different donors simultaneously, but without ensuring coherence and harmonization of approaches of individual assistance projects and actions.

This situation is exacerbated by the fact that donors rarely coordinate their work. Although in some other areas donor agencies increasingly act as partners in comprehensive programs involving several financing and aid-giving agencies, in management and administration most donors still prefer to maintain their identity and pursue their own policy through separate, sometimes even overlapping and competing, projects.

Second, many projects are used to tackle specific practical administrative and managerial issues but contribute little to staff development. Foreign experts and consultants undertake management surveys, design new planning and control schemes, carry out feasibility studies, and give courses, but the involvement of local professionals is insignificant. A job is done, but little is accomplished in the way of developing the capability for doing the same job in the future without turning again to foreign experts. Instead of progressing toward self-reliance, many a country continues to depend on foreign expertise. A continued shortage of high-level manpower and limited absorptive capacity in least developed countries is one cause among many others such as the above-mentioned poor planning and coordination of cooperation projects.

Third, the discrepancy between the real cost of foreign management expertise and the benefits that really come from it is steadily increasing. This cost may be less visible and cause less concern in projects financed by grants, but it becomes obvious when a full market price must be paid by a developing country. Paradoxically, now and again very expensive international consultants are brought in to deal with issues to which their expertise cannot be applied, and they work in logistic and organizational conditions where they are effective for 20-30 percent of their time, at best.

Many developing countries will probably continue to be interested in technical assistance from industrialized countries and international agencies on issues of management and administration. However, they need to rethink this assistance so as to increase its lasting impact, raise its learning effect, and reduce its cost.

Recently, the international community examined the main flows of technical assistance and concluded that direct technical cooperation among the developing countries (TCDC) deserves more attention. The ILO consulted about fifty management institutions on TCDC in management development and also reviewed TCDC actions that have actually taken place among management practitioners and in the education and training of managers and administrators. 18/ More and more practitioners, as well as professional institutions in developing countries, realise that TCDC could help them in adapting management expertise acquired from the industrialized world to local conditions, and in learning more rapidly about new methods and approaches based on the developing countries' own experiences. In this respect, Asia seems to be particularly active; much regional cooperative work has been done under the auspices of the Asian Productivity Organization.

TCDC will never substitute totally for North-South and interregional cooperation in management and administration. Rather, it complements the latter, since it offers certain distinct advantages. For example, instead of dealing with a similar problem separately and for a higher cost, groups of developing countries, or groups of institutions or enterprises from various countries, can do it jointly and thus less expensively. The cultures of many developing countries are similar: this is a great asset in producing and sharing indigenous management models. Also, comparing management and performance standards among developing countries is very useful, since it helps to orient management and administrative efforts to realistic goals and demonstrates what can be achieved even in a developing country.

The ILO and UNDP provide support to cooperation among management development institutions through an interregional project designed for this specific purpose. A new information system on cooperation opportunities, offers, and demands, called "Management Development Referral Service" (MDRS), has been operated by this project since 1981. To generate and disseminate new ideal likely to make cooperation in management development better focused and more effective, this service is being expanded to cover "innovations in management education, training, and development" that occur in institutions in both industrialized and developing countries.

A Strategy for Future Years

In this part of the paper, we have argued that certain fundamental strategic orientations emerge from the multitude of projects, actions, and institutions used by developing countries to build their management and administrative capabilities and to raise management standards in both the public and private sectors. Our review has indicated that, despite the successes, many pitfalls remain and there is an impressive agenda for action for many years to come. Several approaches are possible.

First of all, it is in the interest of every developing country to know where exactly it stands in management and administration. We are not proposing yet more surveys and reports by foreign consultants, but instead recommend self-diagnostic and self-appraisal exercises, by which countries can assess their own management performance; on this basis they can attempt to determine future objectives and confirm or adjust their strategies. Such self-diagnoses should be encouraged; in fact, they should be done periodically, should include an objective evaluation of past achievements, and should lead to the establishment of plans for future action. International comparison is useful; examples of countries that are a step ahead may have a strong motivating effect. Foreign consultants could assist, but should not be allowed to dominate.

Management problems and needs of important development programs and priority sectors require particular attention. Sectoral development studies-- for example, in preparing for investment planning and resource allocation-- should include an assessment of management and managerial manpower in the sector. It is useful, too, to compare management standards of interconnected sectors within a country: balanced development is impossible if poor management in one sector is allowed to hold back sectors with which it interacts.

A strategic approach to assessing and improving management cannot be applied as a unilateral action of a government department or a national management institute. The best results can be obtained only through tripartite action, started and carried through as a joint effort of government authorities, business circles, trade unions, and other interested social organizations. Interaction and collaboration of the private and public sector are essential and responsibilties should be shared. Excessive reliance on governmental initiative and public resources has already retarded the development of managerial capability in too many countries.

A useful platform for enlisting collaboration of the different social groups willing to help has been found in mixed national bodies such as management development councils or foundations. The establishment of such a body is, of course, only an easy initial step. A national council has to address issues regarded as significant by its members, agree on action to be taken, define a limited number of concrete objectives, and make sure that the members commit themselves to implementation.

In many countries, the coordination and harmonization of national management development and improvement efforts need to be stepped up. In particular, this requires better coordination of management development within enterprises and other organizations with programs and services offered by the educational, training, consulting, organization and methods, research, and similar institutions. Every effort should be made to overcome sectoral barriers, to rationalize the national networks of management institutions, and to improve interinstitutional collaboration in dealing with significant issues.

The future strategy for meeting the management challenge needs to be a dynamic and flexible. It needs to reflect the growing interdependence of the industrialized and the developing world, as well as the pace of worldwide technological, economic, and social changes. The objective is not to get closer to management models and standards that at present appear to work satisfactorily in other countries, but to prepare managers and management systems to face the new problems and situations that the future will bring. Creativity, imagination, flexibility, tolerance, and personal drive are the essential qualities that will help managers to cope with tomorrow's changes and challenges.

IV. <u>Management Development: Some Promising Approaches</u>

This part of the paper sketches briefly some promising approaches that characterize the current state of management development in developing countries. Although few of these have yet been widely used, they deserve attention since all innovative efforts and all experiments likely to make management development more relevant to the needs of particular types of organizations in developing countries, and to contribute to higher organizational performance, are worth identifying, evaluating, and disseminating.

Interventions to Improve Management in Organizations

Organizational Excellence: The Goal of Management Development. The goal of management development is to help nudge organizations toward excellence. Research, consulting, education, and training, when properly linked and in the mainstream of management development, promote organizational excellence. One of the most relevant findings of research on excellence is that excellent organizations spend much more effort developing their human resources than do mediocre ones. Furthermore, management development professionals require a validated vision of excellence in order to raise the expectations of managers to the effort necessary to change organizations for the better.

Interest in organizational excellence waxes and wanes; it is now higher than it has been for decades. 19/ Research on excellent organizations shows that they mutate: excellent organizations today are not exactly like the excellent ones of yesteryear. They share some common features: for example, their business is usually to exploit technological frontiers such as the railroads of the 1860s, the auto companies of the first half of our century, and the electronics companies of today. Another thing they have in common is that they are well adapted to the needs and aspirations of their work forces and, paradoxically, this is where they differ from each other, because work forces differ. An excellent Asian company today is likely to be different from an excellent European company. An excellent African company will be well adapted to its own social and cultural environment.

It is the business of management research to find terms that help managers learn and apply the lessons of excellence, and it is the business of management training to find means to accelerate this learning and application. By promising to bring these lessons home, management development professionals excite managers and raise their expectations. Many failures in management development come from success in raising expectations but failure in delivering the goods; the lessons may be irrelevant, or may be about things the managers had learned long ago.

What does an excellent organization look like? Since organizations are invisible, what terms does a management development professional use to describe organizational excellence? After having studied a number of American and Japanese organizations, for example, Pascale and Athos [20]/ recently developed a "seven-s framework," in which a well-performing organization is examined and described under the following main headings: strategy, structure, systems, staff, skills, style, and superordinate goals. The model is not rigorously scientific; its purpose is to describe for the practising managers how a complex organization structures itself and behaves in order to attain a higher level of performance. Such pragmatic models for describing organizations and analyzing the causes of their success or failure are of interest to the practitioners and management development professionals of developing countries.

Measuring the Performance of Management Development

Management development professionals by themselves cannot produce excellent organizations from mediocre ones; the process of change is much too complicated for that. However, the profession has long had a hierarchy of measurement objectives to help it choose intervention techniques and to evaluate how they are working. These evaluation techniques can be used to assess the practical impact of management development interventions carried out by the organizations themselves, by management institutions, or by a combination of both. We must now turn to these levels of evaluation, before looking at some interventions in detail.

Today, effectiveness of management development is thought of as a mix of five "levels" of evaluation criteria (or objectives, which can be used when evaluating interventions), which are already well-known to professional trainers and consultants: (1) attendance, (2) reaction, (3) learning, (4) behavior and application, and (5) results. They are listed in ascending order of importance for client organizations. In practice, many institutions still count only attendance and call that the number of people they "trained." Institutions also tend to measure participant reactions on forms (often called "happiness sheets") useful for evaluating which sessions, topics, or lecturers should be changed.

Measurement of effectiveness nearly always stops here, largely because clients rarely ask for more. Attending and enjoying a course is seen by many managers as a reward for performance or a prerequisite for promotions; sadly, few client organizations and management institutions do much to discourage this notion. For example, more than 80 percent of those management institutions that train public sector managers are co-opted by the career objectives of the public service. An officer wants a number of training courses on his personal data sheet to improve his promotion possibilities. Going to a course is sufficient, but improving performance is irrelevant, because the performance of so few public organizations is measured, let alone people's contribution to it. What is taught is what the teacher knows. What, if anything, is learned is difficult to apply on return to the old job or on assignment to a new one.

The third level of measurement, learning, can be measured with "before and after tests" or by having the participants do exercises that embody what was taught. This is useful for teaching management techniques such as PERT/CPM, work study, reporting procedures, accounting techniques, project design and evaluation, and other technical topics, but is insufficient for developing all the skills that effective managers should have.

Attendance, reaction, and learning can be measured in the classroom. Behavioral change and on-the-job application cannot. Changes in job behavior can only be measured "back home on the job." When a management institution attempts for the first time to measure "back home" application, it usually finds that what was learned was not applied. The institution then realizes that its staff must follow the participants into their organizations in order to help them to change job behavior. Courses are then redesigned to include back home project work. Managers may be admitted to a course only if they have identified a "back home" problem to solve. Such advisory or extension work becomes a form of consultancy to augment training. Thus, institutions that want results must carry out research, consulting, and training and must spend a significant amount of staff time working inside the client organizations. To do so, the institution must revise its policy and change its own behavior. Is it worth it? Do clients in critical sectors expect and appreciate it?

The main difficulty was summed up recently by the director of a strong regional management institute in Africa: "We would like to demonstrate every year that our work contributes to improved performance of national programmes and projects." However, few senior administrators know what goes

on inside their organizations. They are often in politically sensitive
situations and they tell me in private that their organization cannot tolerate
too much change. Thus, to show results we must concentrate on the handful of
senior managers who really want to improve their organizations.

Successful Organizations Take the Initiative

Managers who improve their organizations' performance invest in staff
development. They develop their own training departments and programs and
bring in outside expertise as well. Thus management development interventions
can be best understood by looking at what organizations are doing, and how
they are combining the staff development they "make" (on-the-job coaching, in-
plant training, job rotation, project work, monitoring, and so on) with the
management development they "buy" (open short courses, self-development
packages, sabbaticals, entry-level requirements of graduates from the
education system, and the like.

Currently, the most effective in-service management development is
done by the giant multinationals, such as IBM, Matsushita, General Electric,
or Hewlett-Packard. For example, one of the best staff development processes
is probably that of Matsushita, the world's largest consumer electronics
company, which employs over 200,000 people. Although the company is
decentralized to maintain entrepreneurial drive, it centralises four
functions: accounting, capital budgeting and performance reviews, personnel,
and training. It hires young people who are open and malleable and brings
them up to believe in the company and to live by its rules. The training
system indoctrinates new recruits in the company philosophy and teaches them
about its structure, products, and financial system. On-the-job exposure to
sales and production establishes the basis for life-long competence. At each
promotion, managers and supervisors receive more training in company

philosophy, sales, and production. Each year, 5 percent of the employees (managers, supervisors, and workers) rotate from one division to another. All company professionals begin their training in classrooms and on the job, learning the fundamentals of the company's business. Each professional spends six months working directly in a retail outlet and also performing routine tasks on an assembly line. Such companies do most of their management development themselves. At the same time, they account for more than 80 percent of the work of management institutions.

Companies in competitive sectors such as manufacturing and distribution, in developing and developed countries alike, invest more on the average in staff development than do organizations in monopoly situations such as public utilities and government agencies. Consequently, many people are pessimistic about being able to use management development as a lever to improve the performance of public organizations. There are many fine exceptions, however; some public organizations are shining examples of good staff development. Let us consider two.

Centrais Electricas de Minas Gerais (CEMIG) of Brazil developed an innovative staff selection and development system that seems to account, at least in part, for bottom-line results and high morale. A typical management problem in utilities is that of maintaining an organizational "esprit de corps" in the conditions under which they operate--routinized work, monopoly situation, no new product excitement, and so on. These can all lead to ossification. CEMIG's answer is based on a study of a physician/psychologist that compared the internal structures of organisms and organizations. He identified the organizational analogy of the organism's nervous system as the personnel function (other writers have advocated the information system or the finance department for this role). He noted that the personnel function could help integrate the individual into the organization and thus was responsible

for reducing and eliminating conflicts between the objectives of individuals

and their organization and, by extension, interdepartmental conflicts, and so

on. CEMIG adopted this philosophy, and still applies it as their personnel

policy. This translates into a careful personnel selection process based on a

battery of tests evaluated by psychologists, sociologists, and

anthropologists, followed by updating of the personal profiles thus obtained

during the career of each individual. These profiles are matched with job

descriptions and are used as the basis for preparing short-lists of candidates

for promotion or transfer; for presentation to concerned bosses; as well as

for identifying candidates for training, counseling, and so forth.

Clumsily handled, this process could lead to paternalism or could

degenerate into mechanistic decisions based only on test results, but CEMIG

has avoided these pitfalls and consequently has a long history of industrial

peace. Other Brazilian utilities send their personnel to CEMIG for training

and study tours, and it is one of the few Brazilian power utilities to operate

at a profit.

A second example comes from the Philippines, where the Local Water

Utilities Administration (LWUA) has helped hundreds of municipal water

authorities improve their performance in the past few years. LWUA was

established to break a vicious cycle most countries are caught up in:

customers of most municipal water authorities have forgotten the concept of an

efficient water service. Service is poor because the personnel are

inefficient, the facilities break down often because salaries are low, and

there is no money for repairs because people do not pay because the service is

poor. LWUA was able to break this cycle in hundreds of municipalities by weaning the systems from excessive local politics and helping them to operate in a business-like manner.

To do so, LWUA set up an exemplary management development program for its own staff and for the staff of its clients--the municipal water authorities. LWUA has a rigid screening process and offers attractive compensation packages to young, capable, and motivated engineers. It prefers to recruit fresh graduates to avoid having to help mature engineers unlearn bad habits. These cadet engineers go through a two-month "cadetship training programme" before being fielded. A few years later, each "battle-scarred" engineer returns for a four-month advanced course designed to close the gap between theory and practice. In addition, LWUA uses a variety of other methods to provide staff members at various points of their careers with new knowledge and, in particular, to give them an opportunity to change work attitudes and outlook. Like many other good managers, Carlos Leano, director of LWUA, points out that LWUA uses overseas fellowships to reward good performance and to broaden a person's outlook, not as a substitute for staff development.

An unusual feature of LWUA, which perhaps accounts for much of its success, is the management advisory service it provides. Every month, each municipal water authority is visited by a team of two LWUA advisors who sit with the general managers to solve pressing problems and draw up a plan of action that the advisors monitor on subsequent visits. This service for the 200 or so municipal water authorities under LWUA's wing is based on a "management audit checklist" that incorporates a set of development indicators that reflect the characteristics of well-managed water authorities. Progress toward business-like efficiency is seen as the month-by-month accumulation of points on this checklist. The junior advisers learn their skills largely by being teamed up with senior advisers. This one-on-one training and field experience is supplemented by monthly meetings using case analyses and lectures.

Client training at LWUA is at least as important as internal staff development and the management advisory service. It aims at three audiences: policymakers, water authority managers, and technicians. Seminars for policymakers are designed to help members of communities from different walks of life, who often for the first time in their lives suddenly find themselves making policies for a complex public utility. The seminars are credited with helping these board members find innovative solutions to the age-old water supply problems of their communities. The periodic seminars for management teams from different authorities are considered by LWUA to be among the most exiting in its client training program. The technical training courses cover water quality surveillance, leak detection and repair, equipment operation, and maintenance. In addition, LWUA runs a certification program to increase the number of qualified operators throughout the country. One of the most innovative programs is the preconstruction seminars organized to bring together contractors, construction inspectors, local officials, and interested members of the community prior to any large-scale construction project.

Top Management Action Planning

Various approaches can be used to start meaningful performance improvement and management development programs in an organization and, at the same time, to do it with full involvement of the top management team. The objective is to avoid situations in which top management "tolerates" a program, but regards it as something that does not concern line managers and should be handled only by internal consultants, in-plant trainers, or management services.

The version we will discuss is called "programming (or planning) for improved enterprise performance" (PIP) 21/ ; it has been used by ILO and other organizations in hundreds of enterprises, projects and programs in scores of countries. 22/

PIP essentially helps a top management team prepare and carry out an action plan for improving organizational performance. The heart of the process is a workshop, preceded by a briefing, during which the management team must decide whether PIP is sufficiently promising to justify investing considerable management time and effort. The workshop takes about six days, which can be spread over several weeks. A series of specially designed forms are used to lead the team through problem identification, analysis, objective setting, plan formulation, and implementation planning. When PIP is successful, these forms and procedures become part of the recurrent planning and implementation processes of the management team.

Basically, PIP can be introduced by an organization, public or private, as an internal exercise, without involving any external consultants or trainers. If an organization lacks action planning and organization development expertise, however, external help from an action-oriented management institution may be very useful. In Eastern Nigeria in 1976, for example, the Nigerian Centre for Management Development (CMD) found that the public enterprises that had produced PIP action plans could not implement parts of their plans because of government-imposed restrictions. So the chief executives of the enterprises were encouraged to form an association to define their mutual problems and formulate a common strategy. CMD then assisted the association in holding a two-day meeting with representatives of government, supervisory authorities, and company teams. In the meeting, each group first exchanged its mutual perceptions of each other. The managers, on one hand, thought that the government officials were unduly slow and restrictive in approving financial requests, while at the same time expecting the managers to carry out ambitious expansion plans. The government officials, on the other hand, said that the executives lacked prudence and experience and were too willing to risk government funds. The consultants from CMD controlled this airing of views and kept the meeting task oriented, rather than finger pointing. A plan was agreed upon to grant increasing autonomy to the executives in finance and personnel matters, so that the companies could better accomplish their mandates. This process illustrates a two-stage campaign of using PIP first, then constructive confrontation with authorities later.

Such a dialogue with supervising authorities can also be integrated into the action-planning process so that the rules imposed on companies can be modified and new rules used to improve the plans. When action-planning workshops are held simultaneously on one residential site, the management teams of the different companies learn from each other as they present the partial results of their analyses of their own problems to other executives. They quickly discover their common problems, some of which can best be resolved through joint action. In this style of workshop, government authorities have to be kept out of the internal deliberations of the company teams.

A management institution in an Arab country recently held action-planning workshops simultaneously for six public enterprises, involving government officials only at the beginning and end. The officials were first given the opportunity to describe the great hopes that the government and the people had for the public enterprises and to berate management for not meeting these expectations. The officials were then asked to leave for three days and

invited to return later to hear the action plans of the management teams.
Each team then met separately to develop action plans to meet pressing
needs. They set targets and identified constraints; these included the
lengthy and often irrelevant staff recruitment procedures of the Public
Service Commission, the bureaucratic delays in procuring and stocking spare
parts to keep facilities running, the slow procedures and irrelevant
limitations in the construction and commissioning of new facilities, and the
lack of incentives and disciplinary discretion to accompany the development of
training and career advancement policies. The management consultants helped
each team distinguish the actions they, as managers, could take alone from
those requiring governmental policy changes. Before presenting their plans in
a session attended by government officials, the managers nominated a
"statesman" to present specific proposals. A lively and productive meeting
followed. Some government policies were subsequently modified and management
morale and commitment improved over the next few months. Some senior
ministers were subsequently replaced by professionals more familiar with
public enterprise management. A year later, informal evaluations showed that
several companies were making good progress on reducing costs and improving
productivity and service.

Action-planning interventions, while powerful, must be used
judiciously. Some versions have weaknesses that can be overcome in
combination with other management development techniques. Their power lies in
helping company teams that want to improve move along appropriate paths. In
semicontrolled experimental situations in Nigeria, for example, organizations
that used PIP solved three times as many problems over a six-month period as
those that did not use PIP. The managers in the experimental group said they
had become much more committed to their organizations than before.

However, little evidence yet exists to indicate that action-planning workshops alone improve "bottom-line" performance. Top management action planning can fail if not properly prepared and not based on hard data. Management institutions too often disengage from a client enterprise too soon after it has produced an action plan. Most action plans contain activities such as the design and installation of improved systems for budgeting, financial control, and personnel development, which need consulting assistance. Thus, management teams must see action planning as only one step in a long improvement process, not as a panacea. In their enthusiasm for PIP (or management by objectives, or zero-based budgeting, and so on) institutions and managers too seldom commit themselves to essential follow-up activities. Nonetheless, the process of guiding a top management team through a problem-solving process is usually preferable to the prevailing approaches of merely hiring consultants or sending managers to courses.

Whether top management action planning alone produces bottom-line results is considered an irrelevant issue by some. Herbert Simon once pointed out that trying to trace the influence of an intervention on profit, sales, market share, and the like, is like trying to detect the change in the water flowing over Niagara Falls caused by a rainstorm in Northern Minnesota: something has undoubtedly changed, but when and by how much may be unimportant in the larger scheme of things.

By putting technological content into the action-planning process, a management institution can help solve ciritical technological transfer problems. The ILO, for example, organized several action-planning workshops with road engineers to help them choose and implement an appropriate mix of technologies for constructing and maintaining rural feeder roads. 23/ The workshops start with a session on the status and specific problems of rural

road management in the given country and proceed to detailed presentations on
the most successful road programs, followed by an analysis of the pros and
cons of different approaches. The second half begins when most participants
have become interested in finding out what they would have to do to implement
a different technological mix. Then they engage in exercises based on the
difficulties usually encountered in switching technologies, such as planning a
pilot project; setting up a supervisory training program; selecting, training,
and paying casual labour; and specifying and procuring good tools and
equipment. 24/ The final output of such workshops are action plans for pilot
projects. A measure of success is whether the participants are able to
produce a credible action plan, possibly for the external funding of a pilot
project to test workable combinations of technology and organization.

Inovations in Management Education and Training

The previous section described how to generate and implement
performance improvement programs aimed at specific organizational problems,
management systems, and practices. To focus on action taken by organizations
does not mean, however, that less management education and training will be
needed in the future. Classroom training provides knowledge and skills that
will ensure practical improvements. Performance improvement programs in
organizations do not reduce training needs, but help organizations to become
more selective in sending their personnel to external training programs and
also in designing their own in-plant and in-service training. Good courses
can precede or supplement performance improvement actions, stimulate the
managers' interest in doing things better, and increase their problem-solving
and communication skills.

Not only the relevance and quality of the course content, but also
organization and methodology greatly influence the effectiveness of

training. Several factors call for innovations in management training in developing countries:

(1) The millions of managers who need basic and advanced training;

(2) The growing cost of training programs, which makes good training less and less accessible to those organizations that need it most;

(3) Logistical problems, such as great distances and poor communications, mainly affecting managers in remote ' areas.

(4) The need for new attitudes and behavioral changes, which is difficult to achieve with certain types of training (for example, passive listening to lectures), but can be assisted by other types of active and participative training;

(5) The dynamism of managers themselves, that is, of their work techniques, practices, and theories: managers must have an opportunity to bring themselves up to date and exchange experience, even if working in difficult conditions and locations in a developing country.

Management development professionals have long recognized the shortcomings, such as the lack of the on-the-job applications, of short courses (often because too few people from one organization attend a course to support changing the way things are done), or the irrelevance of course content (often because too little effort was put into to finding out the needs of participants). In the next few sections we examine several approaches that have been used to overcome such shortcomings and that have had a measure of success. In these descriptions we stress several points: first, most successful approaches control the selection of participants to ensure success; second, they make the participants co-responsible for designing the training program and controlling its delivery; and third, they emphasize the process of learning and practical application.

An overriding feature of all successful approaches to management development is an intensive search for maximum relevance to work situations: the objective is to make the managers think about what they can improve and to really start some action.

Tailored Programs

Not only do standard courses take insufficient account of specific problems of various organizations from which participants come, but also most organizations complain that managers usually return from such courses with unrealistically high expectations and a set of management tools that cannot be applied. One way of reducing this "re-entry" problem is to tailor training programs and packages to particular enterprises or government agencies. This can be achieved by adapting standard packages or modular materials. In developing countries, however, fewer than one trainer in ten has the skills or incentives to tailor training to the needs of particular organizations. A recent examination of accounting courses for managers of water agencies showed that almost all the examples and exercises were from manufacturing firms. As one senior training specialist recently put it, "Most trainers, like many university professors, will continue to use the same old materials and examples for decades unless they are given the opportunity to test their methods in the real world to change behavior and improve organizational performance."

Training cases and in-basket exercises based on an organization's actual business situation are commonly used for tailoring. Project management trainers at Western Carolina University, for example, 25/ create in-basket exercises to adapt project management training to each company's specific needs. This approach is well suited to the almost universal problem of helping new engineers learn rapidly their management tasks. Most project-oriented companies find that their main management development problem is how to speed up the rate at which engineers learn to manage projects on the job. Consequently, these companies create a high demand for short, two- to five-day training seminars and workshops on management techniques (conflict management, negotiation techniques, planning and control methods, and so on) carefully adapted to the project situation. Currently, this demand is met primarily by "canned" generalized packages, which at best encourage an open discussion of management concerns and an exposure to management theory, and from which little back-home application can be expected.

To improve this back-home application, the Western Caronlina faculty creates in-basket exercises as case studies of projects drawn from a company's files. Prior to conducting a course, a trainer/consultant visits the company and selects situations from company files that reflect its main training needs; he creates a coherent set of exercises to mesh with the standard handouts and readings that cover project management topics. Ideally, the participants include prospective project managers, experienced managers, and reprersentatives of various staff departments in the company. This type of mix facilitates an exchange of views across the organization, so that the participants can provide each other with immediate feedback about each other's ideas for dealing with problems and defining acceptable behavior.

The ILO construction project management training activities use a similar approach. Short courses are based on a basic text 26/ and a set of locally customized cases and exercises. The current emphasis in the program is to help trainers and consultants from institutions in each country to develop their own cases and exercises from the project problems of that country and to exchange these materials periodically.

Practical exercises and cases, which are based on research into local problems, are two of the many methods of improving the ratio of effectiveness to cost. Two broad types of cost are of concern here: the one-time cost of doing the research and developing and testing the materials, and the repetitive costs of delivering the training to batch after batch of trainees. In-basket exercises and teaching cases raise both the one-time cost as well as the effectiveness of training, compared with the conventional lectures and discussion. Fortunately, the effectiveness of these newer methods more than outweights their cost. Effectiveness is high for several reasons: managers become more involved in the learning process when they recognize a familiar problem; they are more likely to learn from other managers who have faced similar problems; and they are more likely to see how they can apply what they learned back on the job.

A tailor-made program can be prepared and organized by an enterprise using its own training resources, particularly if line and staff managers are able and prepared to act as trainers. Many companies, however, want to enhance their internal experience by external inputs from management institutions. More and more programs of this type are being designed as joint ventures between one or a group of companies and a management school or center. In some centers, such programs account for 40-50 percent of the total volume of their training activity.

Campaign-type, Action-oriented Programs

A campaign-type, action-oriented program is one that makes a special effort over a defined period of time to tackle a significant practical problem, mobilizing fairly large management teams and, as a rule, requiring considerable resources. The interventions have to be extended long enough for bottom-line results to become visible or striking.

A good example of a campaign is the "training-through-consultancy" program that the National Productivity Centre (NPC) of Ethiopia 27/ has been using since 1979 to help scores of manufacturing companies solve maintenance problems. The program has several features that can be adopted elsewhere. It was developed in response to a precise request from the Minister of Industry, who was keen to increase production, reduce down-time and scrapping, and improve product quality in several dozen factories. In responding to this mandate, NPC realized that it lacked sufficient consultants to keep up with growing problems in the factories. Also, they found managers hesitant and uncommitted to implementing their recommendations. NPC decided to increase the number and capability of consultant-managers from within the companies.

The program starts with short seminars for top managers and policymakers, during which hundreds of maintenance problems are aired. Then top managers nominate maintenance managers from within the companies to participate in long courses on solving maintenance problems. After a few weeks of studying cases and improving their problem-solving skills, maintenance managers form closely supervised teams to undertake team consultancy assignments. The course leaders take care not to lecture too much. Participants are encouraged to request information when they need it to solve a problem. Certificates of completion (not attendance!) are awarded to members of the teams when their recommendations are "signed off" by plant management. Then the participants carry out individual consultancy assignments in their own factories in collaboration with a "vertical slice" of their own companies, that is, with managers and operators at each level in each company who have already received training in maintenance and are prepared to work in teams to solve problems.

NPC documents and closely monitors implementation of recommendations in the plants. It produces "emulation" tables and guidelines to show managers which plants are best at improving maintenance. These factories serve as models from which managers from other plants can learn. At the certificate award ceremonies, the best consulting teams describe their accomplishments to the Minister of Industry, and the best plant managers describe how they have implemented improvements.

Thus, NPC's role is balanced between training, consulting, coaching, and monitoring implementation of recommendations. Rather than just evaluate the program at its end, NPC uses continuous evaluation to adjust and improve the program as it expands. Evaluation has documented savings of at least eight times the cost of the program, in which more than 1,000 people received training and 20 maintenance management consultants were certified. NPC finds that managers' attitudes towards maintenance have changed. Cooperation between production and maintenance departments in most plants is better. Down-time has been reduced between 7 and 15 percent; record keeping and plant layouts are better. In 1982, four among the participating enterprises documented annual savings of more than $1.2 million from increased production, prolonged machine life, increased numbers of spare parts produced locally, and reduced rejection of production. In the same year, NPC expanded the program to 143 factories. NPC finds it needs not claim credit for these achievements; corporation executives and ministry officials willingly share the credit for

these improvements with NPC. This same program design is now being adapted
and replicated in Ethiopia to other pinpointed priority problems, such as
production management, quality assurance, product development, and customer
service.

Business Clinics

This approach combines some elements of top management action
planning described in section 3.1 with a campaign approach. Instead of
working only with top management teams from different types of enterprises, it
is used with groups of senior managers of enterprises in the same industry
(transport, insurance, and so on); and rather than focusing on one type of
pinpointed improvement (such as maintenance management), it focuses on overall
improvement by training the managers to analyze many performance indicators in
sessions called "business clinics" based on "interfirm comparison."

In the Philippines, for example, the ILO recently started providing
advisory services to owners and operators of bus and truck companies to help
them reduce their operating costs. The heart of this service, the business
clinic, is held monthly for the managers of transport companies facing similar
problems. The leader of each business clinic is a consultant trained by an
ILO/DANIDA regional project to use programable calculators to compute
technical and financial performance ratios, such as "tyre cost per thousand
kilometres," or "fuel cost per thousand kilometres", for each participating
firm.

To participate, a company must agree to provide the consultant with
the data necesssary to compute the ratios. Prior to the clinic, each company
receives a report showing its ratios and comparisons with typical companies in
the group. During the clinic, the managers compare their ratios and exchange
suggestions about how to improve their ratios. Some companies, for example,

decided to expand driver training to reduce the cost of fuel and tyres; they formed a group to buy tyres in quantity. One company that was initially at the bottom in terms of performance ratios started an efficiency campaign and, within a month, had moved up among the best-managed companies.

Interfirm comparison can be converted to intrafirm comparison and used to develop the management skills in large organizations that provide homogenous services, such as public utilities. In 1980, the Centre for Management Development (CMD) in Nigeria set up such a management development system for the Nigerian Electricity Power Authority (NEPA). CMD consultants collected financial and operating data for the nineteen state districts throughout Nigeria to which NEPA provides electric power. These data, processed by computer, were converted into a pyramid of comparable performance indicators, mostly ratios. Then an action-planning workshop was held, similar to the PIP workshops described earlier, during which the management teams compared performance ratios, exchanged ideas on how to improve performance, and prepared action plans to improve selected ratios. The response of the managers was enthusiastic: they claimed they had gained significant insight into how to improve the management of their districts.

Management institutions that accept the premise that managers learn best from each other are ideally placed to organize business-clinic services based on interfirm comparisons. Because the results of the business-clinic style of interventions can be measured in terms of changes in "bottom line" performance indicators, the enterprises are in a good position to share credit for improved performance with management institutions that help organize such business clinics. Consequently, there is a trend among management development professionals to package business-clinic approaches, and we can expect to see them used more in the future. But this approach works only under certain conditions. Since the participating managers share and compare performance indicators on the basis of their own organizations' operating figures, they must be willing to open their books at least to the consultants who organize the service. Cultures in which managers are naturally secretive are poor places to demonstrate this approach, as are sectors where trade secrets are the basis for competition for the same market. In contrast, medium and large farmers, small and medium retailers and transporters, and public utilities appear to be ideal candidates.

Modular Approach to Management Training

The preceding examples have demonstrated approaches that achieve results at different levels--from participant response through on-the-job application to the bottom line--and therefore they deserve to be packaged to enhance their chances and reduce the cost of their being more widely applied.

Modular packaging is the principal way to reduce the cost of customizing training and consulting to fit the needs of particular industries or firms. By using modular programs, trainers need develop fewer materials from scratch. Furthermore, many recent modular packages produced for developing countries are based on the latest validated methodologies about how adults learn. 28/ Existing training institutions, by contrast, are often locked into using outdated materials and methods that rely heavily on lecturing and certificate-granting, which rarely translate into on-the-job improvements. Thus the modular packages can considerably improve the quality of the programs of many institutions.

The ILO Management Development Programme published its first major modular program in 1981 as the "Modular programme for supervisory development." The modules are grouped under four headings: Introduction (2 modules); Supervisory techniques (11 modules); The main supervisory areas

(8 modules); and Supervising people (13 modules). They include a learning

text for the trainee, detailed guidelines for trainers, case studies,

practical exercises, questions for discussions, suggestions for reading, and

action guidelines. The production of this package was preceded by a study of

more than 100 supervisory training programs from industrialized and developing

countries that reflected the practical training experience available

throughout the world, and it was discussed with leading trainers in industry

and training institutions. The program is already being used in several

different ways to train supervisory development trainers and to tailor

programs for sectors and companies. Some organizations find it useful also

for middle management training. Several regional and national workshops for

trainers have been organized to help in using the package and adapting it to

local needs. Formal evaluation is now underway.

The "Materials and techniques for co-operative management training"

(MATCOM) now consist of six integrated training packages based on the well-

researched training needs of managers of producer or marketing cooperatives.

The draft packages were extensively field tested and the test results used to

produce general packages, which were printed and distributed to national

training institutions, particularly to cooperative training centers. Local

adaptation is encouraged, and at least part of the materials now exist in

fourteen languages. The materials describe what the trainees should do,

session by session. Nineteen self-study booklets have been produced. To

emphasize on-the-job application, the materials include "action commitment"

sections to encourage trainees to plan solutions to certain problems they face

at work. In consultation with other trainees and the trainer, each trainee

works out a detailed plan to which he is committed. So far, more than 80

pilot training exercises have been run, more than 300 trainers trained, and

more than 1,000 staff and managers have attended courses using the modular
package.

Thus far, impact evaluations have been carried out in six
countries. A sample of 100 managers completed post-course questionnaires. Of
these, two-thirds stated that their performance had improved as a result of
the training, and most respondents were able to cite examples of how the
program had helped them to reduce costs or improve service. The evaluation
uncovered problems typical of modular packages. They tend to be little used
and to sit on shelves unless provision is made for changing the aims and
philosophy of the training institutions. Established curricula and a bias
toward the lecture method limit their use and adaptation. Lecturers in
established training institutions rarely have practical experience; they treat
management in the only way they know--as a theory. Lecturers are evaluated on
classroom performance, not on on-the-job applications. Although the MATCOM
materials encourage action commitment, few co-operative training institutions
have the time, budget allocations, or procedures to do necessary follow up.
Thus, the production of modular materials is only an early step in reforming
management development. Pilot results must be demonstrated with the clients
and mutual accountability between clients and institutions gradually built up
to turn "teaching factories" based on tutor-directed, child-oriented
methodologies, into true management development institutions.

In contrast to MATCOM, the "Modules for the training of supervisors
for labor-based road construction and maintenance" are based on the principle
that successful development programs (for example, Kenya's Rural Roads
Program, or the Philippines Rice Self-sufficiency Program), are almost always
the result of the adaptation of locally appropriate technology and
management. Successful programs seem to grow only from well-tested pilot

projects. This package is part of a training and advisory system that responds to a priority need: countries are unable to construct and maintain rural road networks within available budgets when they use the conventional technologies and administrative structure. Thus, the content of the road supervisory training modules is based largely on materials from successful, long-running, labor-based road projects in Kenya, the Philippines, and elsewhere. The modular format, however, encourages adaptation to local conditions; it contains specific instructions for trainer and trainee-supervisor alike. It is designed to be delivered through trainee-selection systems similar to those in the few successful rural road programs. When adapted, it offers a means of transferring technology and administration from one country to another. Preliminary evaluations show that the package works well with little modification in countries where road construction supervisors are somewhat literate. Different training approaches may be required where literacy rates are low.

Manager Self-development

It could be argued that any management development is mainly self-development: after all, it is the trainee who decides in the end whether he will learn, retain, and use what is made available to him in various forms through training programs. Manager self-development approaches emphasize this feature so that the main decisions concerning what to learn, how, at what pace, in cooperation with whom, and so on are more in the hands of the manager himself. Self-development may in fact be a misleading term, conjuring up as it does the image of an individual burning the midnight oil with self-improvement books and correspondence courses. To make this type of training work, organizations and management institutions have to set up favorable learning situations and help managers by preparing and distributing good training materials.

Self-development approaches deserve particular attention in the developing regions, where they can reduce the cost of management training, and can help people realize that everyone should feel responsible for his own development and that no manager should wait passively to be developed by somebody else. It is particularly difficult to develop these new attitudes to learning in countries where traditional cultures and bureaucratic structures may discourage dynamism and personal initiative.

A wide variety of self-development methods and materials are emerging, often in combination with traditional, teacher-centered training programs. Some examples are found in a number of public and private enterprises and in local government in the United Kingdom, where managers have established self-development groups in which they (1) learn and practi,e individual self-development techniques; (2) learn to look at themselves and their personal problems and improvement prospects; and (3) work on real work and life issues and exchange experience. Such approaches are being adopted in developing countries as well. The Mananga Agricultural Management Centre in Swaziland, which caters to agricultural managers from a score of countries, starts each long course with self-assessment instruments. Having assessed his own development priorities, each participant is guided through a set of courses, projects, and readings adapted to his individual needs.

"Instructor-free training" (IFT) is an example of a training system based on self-development principles and suited to creating behavioral change in a group by putting both the content and the motivating methodology into the system. It has been validated by companies, such as Xerox and Standard Bank, in Europe as well as in Africa. IFT uses a combination of video-cassette, workbook, and leader's guide. The leader is usually a member of a natural work group who is responsible for keeping the group moving along. Typical IFT programs concentrate on how to improve meetings, define jobs, set targets, and appraise personal performance. Each program has up to four sessions, and lasts about fifteen hours, depending on the progress of the group. A program starts with a filmed example of a poorly managed common situation; the group then analyzes the situation and discusses how the situation could be improved. Then they watch a filmed reenactment of the situation that points out the skills and principles to use in improving the situation. The group progresses through sessions in which they practise the skills and plan how they will apply them on the job. By means of the natural work groups, an IFT program can rely on peer pressure to reinforce the use of the skills. By combining the training into self-contained packages, IFT can reduce the classroom demand on skilled trainers, freeing them to work on needs analysis, planning, evaluation, and coaching.

"Action learning" is a popular method of manager self-development in many industrialized and developing countries but is not yet practiced on a large scale. In most cases, the manager undertakes a special project, individually or in a small group, to work on specific problems in his organization. Managers from different organizations may cooperate in defining these problems and exchanging experience on the solutions that are proposed, as well as on the best way to implement them.

In Nigeria, manager self-development methods are used in training programs for senior and middle managers organized by the Borno and Kano state governments. Eight programs, lasting twelve weeks and involving twenty-five participants each, have been organized over the past three years. Each program starts with a short introductory period using mainly traditional methods. In the third week, self-development techniques are used almost exclusively. Its main features are: (1) abstract theory and lecturing are minimized; (2) a great deal of work is done in pairs and small groups addressing real-life problems faced by the participants and their organizations; (3) participants receive specific instruction on how to learn, develop, and apply various self-diagnosis and self-improvement techniques; (4) self-diagnostic material is used and supplemented by advice and coaching when necessary; (5) two weeks are devoted to team work on a complex problem concerning several organizations, and conclusions are presented to a panel of high-level government officials.

The behavioral change and the practical results achieved are evaluated six to twelve months after the completion of the program, mainly through an interview with the participants' chiefs. The program had a positive effect on the self-confidence of individuals--their ability to communicate with others, speak in public, make decisions, and critically evaluate experience. From the point of view of the organization, improvements have been found in understanding and handling more complex problems involving several departments. Several problems, which in the past would have been tackled in a bureaucratic way (by merely reporting to higher authority) were resolved by the direct collaboration of individuals from several departments.

A great advantage of these and other self-development approaches is that they do not separate the manager's work life and work problems from his whole life, including family and social life. Nevertheless, productive self-development requires excellent preparation and, although trainers may not be directly involved, they have to prepare high quality self-development materials and may have to be available for broad guidance, advice, and coaching.

Electronics and Management Development

The impact, both potential and actual, of electronics on management development is tremendous. Developing countries with a stable supply of electricity and reasonable maintenance and repair services can gain great advantages. Furthermore, the recent explosive growth in the market for micro and minicomputers in industrialized countries has opened new possibilities. Although the value of installed computers in most developing countries has not increased much since 1980, the number of small computers, and hence the number of people who have access to them, has increased severalfold. Because electronic technology affects most functions of enterprise management--production, marketing, distribution, research, finance, and accounting--the technological changes should be seen from three interacting viewpoints: the impact of electronics on management development, its impact on how managers manage, and the problems of managing and effectively utilizing the electronic resources themselves.

Electronics is revolutionizing the functions of management development: training, consulting, and research. Electronic aids, such as computers, videotapes, and videodiscs, can significantly improve both the way the training content is delivered and how the training process is monitored and controlled. The early advocaters of computer-assisted instruction (CAI) saw computers as delivering instruction. The great tide of CAI enthusiasm, which crested in the 1970s, has subsided and left behind a few puddles of scattered devotees; but now the arrival of smaller, cheaper machines has engendered a CAI revival. In the meantime, however, we have learned much more about how adults learn and how to help them apply what they have learned; so we can better avoid the mistakes of the CAI movement.

Most of the problem stemmed from the misguided use of electronics; for example, most CAI applications concentrated on using computers to instruct, thus turning them into very expensive page turners. The training community has now learned that computer technology cannot effectively replace all the trainer's traditional functions. A typical effective computer-based. teaching-learning package is designed so that the learner reads some text from a manual and then is instructed to go to a machine to do some exercises that help him apply what he has learned and build skill in applying it. Each exercise takes from 15 to 45 minutes to work. In this way, the computer becomes a tool for individualizing instruction, permitting students to work at their own pace, and often at their own work site.

Not only are microcomputers becoming far more accessible in developing countries, but since they cannot be divorced from video equipment, they also hold the promise of making some forms of management training much less costly and more effective. Learning packages are now appearing that combine workbooks, textbooks, videotape or disk, instructors' guides, and evaluation systems that have significant advantages over traditional courseware. The workbooks contain the instructions to guide the trainee through a series of practical tasks, experiments, and exercises through which he discovers the essence of what he is expected to learn. The instructors' guide provides technical background to answer questions raised by the trainees (model answers, supplementary explanations) as well as practical advice on how to conduct the course. Such courseware is often superior to the more common teacher-centered courseware because learners are better able to study at their own pace and their interest is more likely to be kept alive than when the teacher is the sole dispenser of knowledge. Also, since the information, the incentives, and the evaluation scheme are embodied in the materials, the role

of instructors is changed from that of experts to that of advisers, whose
function is to keep learners progressing.

Instruction is not synonymous with training, however. Indeed, the
most effective management training is not at all comparable to instruction in
a discipline such as medicine or engineering. Research indicates that
computers are best at improving the effectiveness of an already good training
package, especially on topics where managers must be numerate in order to
solve problems and allocate resources. In these topics, trainees are
instructed through texts (often programmed), video-based cases, and lectures,
and then use a computer-based exercise to consolidate their skill.

Through the use of games and simulations, for example, branch
managers in many international companies are trained to spend their allotted
budgets so as to produce the best return. In some programs, the managers read
a special text on advertising and are then divided into teams to play an
advertising management game. Each team is given a description of a branch
office and its potential market, an economic forecast, and a marketing
budget. Each team prepares a quarterly plan and gives it to the trainer, who
may use a computer program to evaluate it. The teams may also type their plan
on the computer and get their results on the terminal screens. They receive
reports showing the volume of business they have obtained in the quarter. The
teams repeat this cycle for several simulated quarters. Their objective is to
make decisions to sell the most volume across all product lines by the end of
the "year." Without computer support such training games are often unwieldy
and time consuming to play and evaluate; the important element of making
decisions under time pressure is often lost when the consequences of team
decisions must be computed manually. Furthermore, complex calculations may be

necessary to make the exercise sufficiently realistic to be relevant to the job.

The ILO Management Development Program has developed packages on finance and accounting for managers of water and other public utilities. The packages use microcomputer-based simulations to complement quizzes, case studies, lecture notes, and exercises. At the same time, the packages are not dependent on the availability of a computer, and they can be used effectively where computers are not available. When a computer is available and used properly in a training situation, however, the package is likely to be more effective than without a computer. These packages are based on the concept of self-development, which was discussed earlier.

Computer technology for offices and factories is best taught by means of computer-based course software, for here the "medium" and the "message" are closely linked. Computer-based simulations and games are also useful for teaching some aspects of production management, project management, finance and accounting, distribution management, and so forth, because the computer can quickly demonstrate the consequences of decisions based on certain techniques.

But computer-based courseware is expensive to produce: it takes 50 to 100 hours to develop one hour of presentation time, compared with the 20 to 30 hours of development work required per hour of course time in good conventional courses. Such development costs are easiest to justify in institutions and organizations that have to train thousands of students; where content is standardized and highly specialized (so that few qualified teachers are available); where there is a high turnover of trainers and there are many remote sites (with proper facilities), so that it makes more sense to bring the training materials to the trainees than vice versa. With the falling cost of microprocessor technology, such packages are likely to become ever more accessible to developing countries.

Not only can computer-based training software (courseware) represent large investments, but also those investments often result in small benefits when the assumptions on which the courseware was produced fail to materialize. Of particular importance are assumptions about how managers learn best, especially when they come from different cultural backgrounds and have different educational experiences. Most young Third World managers are still people who have learned largely by rote, not by discovery, while older managers generally suffer from inadequate academic backgrounds and have little interest in reading. They share with many managers from industrialized countries a fear of terminals and keyboards. Thus most packages, to be successful, must include time for and material on "learning how to learn." For example, packages that require managers to enter their decisions on a terminal keyboard should include preparatory exercises to help the managers learn their way around the keyboard.

Where computers are concerned, most of ILO's management development effort in the past fifteen years has been in helping managers make proper use of computers. In most developing countries, computers represent significant investments that one tries to use wisely. The analysis usually starts with the recognition that less than, say, 20 percent of the computer capacity in a country is used and that most of the applications are designed to save clerical labor (payroll, accounting, statistics, and so on), while there is high unemployment and a great need to make better use of scarce capital (for example, in transport scheduling or inventory control). Many argue that existing computers are poorly utilized because too few managers understand their potential (hence the need for appreciation courses for managers), and that there are too few systems analysts and programmers (hence the need for courses to train these professionals). On the basis of this type of analysis, ILO has assisted in establishing a score of national centers in countries as diverse as Iraq, Israel, Romania, Sri Lanka, and Tunisia. These efforts have suffered from various problems, including noncompetitive salary scales for experienced systems analysts and insufficient motivation for maximum utilization of expensive equipment.

One of the interesting attempts to overcome these problems was started in 1978 at the National Institute of Business Management (NIBM) of Sri Lanka in setting up a computer-based reporting system for managers of twenty public enterprises. 29/ The system that NIBM set up was based on the then existing system by which the corporations reported to their supervising ministry about their operations (production, sales, absenteeism, cash flow, and the like). Such systems, used by most ministries, share certain problems: corporations find the reports burdensome to prepare, and they generally report late, incompletely, or not at all; similarly, ministry staff often find it too difficult to compile useful information from what the corporations submit.

NIBM designed a computer system to reduce these problems and then trained staff from interested corporations and the ministry to use it. The system was conceived to increase the accuracy and reduce the burden of preparing the input data for the ministry, to spot problems, and to make better decisions. Some corporation managers adopted the new system with enthusiasm, but others did not. So far, there is little evidence that it has brought about substantial improvements in corporate performance. There is ample evidence, however, to show that the training being provided is helping many young people become qualified in the computer field and find rewarding employment.

Trends in the Development of Entrepreneurship

As emphasised in Part II, entrepreneurship is key to development. It is important to see what is being done, and what can be done better, to stimulate entrepreneurship in developing countries, particularly through the creation and sustenance of small and medium enterprises and also the maintenance and enhancement of entrepreneurial attitudes and behavior in society at large.

Reputedly, one of the most successful programs in the developing world is the Entrepreneurship Development Programme (EDP) of the Gujarat State in India. [30/] Started in 1969 to provide capable entrepreneurs with financial backing, the program has expanded to over 70 centers and encompasses most of the components of entrepreneurship support: entrepreneurship selection, training, project identification, assistance in securing finance, infrastructure and related services, and progress evaluation. The program claims to have trained more than 4,000 entrepreneurs, who have started more than 1,500 factories. Untrained entrepreneurs failed seven times as frequently as the ones it trained (21.4 percent as against 3.57 percent); the trained ones were more often profitable (76 percent as against 57 percent) and the bigger their enterprises, the higher their return on investment. Although the program costs about US$150 to train each person, much of the cost is subsidised, so a trainee pays only a token fee.

Each person who enters the EDP is screened by tests and interviews to ensure that he possesses traits associated with successful entrepreneurship. This testing is based on McClelland's theories of achievement motivation. People who demonstrate these traits and have some commercial or industrial experience are likely to be accepted. Those with industrial experience are offered an evening program lasting ninety days, while those without such experience, for example, recent graduates and the educated unemployed, attend a six-month full-time course.

Each program has four main topical areas: achievement motivation, product selection and project development, business management, and practical work experience. First the trainees spend five days on achievement motivation; here the program attempts to increase the trainee's capacity to take initiative, his desire to achieve results, and his ability to define realistic goals. Then, the program moves on parallel tracks where the trainee investigates a viable industrial opportunity while learning the techniques of management. Trainees talk with many people who have industrial and commercial experience to find commercial opportunities and then produce reports covering product-line, market mix, and commercial feasibility. The business management syllabus, which is covered while the trainees search for business opportunities, includes all important aspects of managing and developing a small and medium business enterprise.

Whereas the Gujarat program emphasizes individual entrepreneurs, who can employ on the average five workers, other recent programs emphasize group projects that may stand a better change of creating viable new enterprises. Many of these are associated with large companies in industrialized countries, where technological change and industrial restructuring have put many people with industrial skills out of work at the same time that there is a need to create a whole new generation of enterprises.

Rank Xerox, a multinational in the office equipment sector, has been reducing its staff for several years. Rather than just abandoning redundant employees, Rank Xerox offers to help them set up their own businesses. 31/ A few, whose services are especially vital, become contractors or consultants to Xerox. The company's support to its ex-employees-cum-entrepreneurs has

evolved ad hoc. It offered courses on starting businesses to the 120 or so
employees who wanted them. Many of the new entrepreneurs who attended the
courses formed an association to exchange information on business methods,
goods and services, and price advantages on volume purchasing. Many of the
people, knowing Xerox's needs, sell their products and services to their old
employer. Xerox, in turn, has set up a business support center to provide
services small businesses cannot afford alone—such as conference rooms,
desks, photocopiers, and communication equipment.

The Xerox example illustrates a combination of trends, more highly
developed in some societies, only just appearing in others. For example,
industrial subcontracting is highly developed in Japan. Companies like Honda
and Sony have several hundred thousand small suppliers of components to whom
they provide support and consultancy services. Rather than simply purchase
what suppliers offer, these companies have teams that advise suppliers on how
to improve quality, cut costs, and stay competitive with their other
suppliers. 32/ One is struck by the similarity between this service and the
management and training services that LWUA in the Philippines provides to its
clients, the local water authorities.

Rationally designed business start-up services are rare. One of the
most interesting is a new entrepreneurship program that started in late 1982
in the United Kingdom. There, participants are selected from large businesses
that are reducing their employment, as in the Xerox case. Proto-entrepreneurs
are screened, as in the Gujarat model, but are treated as proto-teams, not
individual entrepreneurs, and the training is physical, with less emphasis on
report writing. Early in the program the teams are given real tasks—for
example, to produce a mailing or to assemble a product. Wherever possible,
"labor" is brought in and the teams' task is to organize it to produce the

work. Afterwards, they discuss how they organize to get the job done. Then, the teams are presented with product ideas and taught how to research their market, contact financing agencies, and create a business entity. Early reports indicate that the businesses created by this process quickly grow to employ twenty to forty people. The main problem the organizers are encountering in this program, however, is that proto-entrepreneurs rarely trust each other; thus it is difficult to create these team-based enterprises.

The speed with which the new enterprises take off is sometimes surprising. In 1981, the Australian government asked several universities there to help create export-oriented companies. Applicants were screened and the courses started with product ideas--inventions--that researchers had come up with but had not yet commercialized, such as sheepskin shoes and articifial insemination for sheep. The participants formed teams and went through a "simulated" process of investigating their market, obtaining finance, and setting up a company. The leaders of one such university program were shocked to find that their program was not a simulation; within three weeks the shoe team had export orders for 40,000 pairs of shoes.

To assist in developing entrepreneurship and improving the performance of small firms in the construction sector of African countries, the ILO has organized the drafting of "Guidelines for the development of small-scale contractors." 33/ This was preceded by country studies of various models for supporting small African contractors. 34/

In Kenya, for example, a National Construction Company (now a parastatal corporation) was set up in 1967 to assist African contractors by providing credit facilities, advisory services, and training. It was also to help contractors obtain work, especially in the public sector. By 1978-79, NCC was giving loans to 53 African contractors, whereas when the NCC started, very few African contractors existed. In Swaziland, the Small Enterprise Development Company (SEDCO) created in 1970 had similar objectives to those of NCC, except that they embraced all types of small-scale industries, not just construction. The extension of SEDCO's training, advisory, and loan services to the construction industry arose in response to the initiative of a few Swazi contractors. In 1980-81, assistance was given on contract with seven times the amount of the loan fund, which then stood at approximately US$434,000. In Botswana, the Botswana Enterprise Development Unit (BEDU) was created in 1974. Although similar in principle to SEDCO, it never possessed the autonomy of a corporation, but has always been a line department of the Ministry of Commerce and Industry. It has provided advisory and training services to contractors, but because it is a government department, its financial help has been much more restricted than that of NCC or SEDCO. The Ghana Bank for Housing and Construction (GBHC) started operations in 1973 with the objective of financing and implementing housing and civil engineering schemes of all kinds. Coupled with this financial objective, however, the Bank was required to develop and promote efficiency in the construction industry generally. The GBHC has been more successful in achieving its financial objective then in improving contractor efficiency.

The country studies and the draft guidelines were submitted to a collective review by representatives of the contractors, as well as of banks, ministries of construction or public works, employers' organizations, and other interested parties form a number of African countries. The resulting guidelines therefore reflect collective experience and wisdom. A systems approach is their prominent feature. They include a wide range of suggestions concerning the revision of the total system in which small contractors are supposed to operate and make their enterprises grow. This includes policies to improve access to work, improve the business environment, provide training and technical advice that is likely to lead to action, organize small contractors' associations, and make development agencies that support small contractors more productive.

As for educating youth in entrepreurship, a promising approach is to link vocational training with some entrepreneurial training. This can be done through various types of programs, depending on the profiles of the participants and the real opportunities for starting a business after students have completed a vocational training program. The ILO is actively experimenting in this area. In Malawi, such a program has been introduced at the National Institute for Vocational, Managerial and Entrepreneurial Training. Participants are selected, through an elaborate process, from rural village communities. Two programs are expected to be operational in the long run. One addresses former graduates who have demonstrated their technical skills (for example, by working for a boss for a number of years) and who would like to start their own small business. The school would provide a package of entrepreneurial and managerial training, including actual start-up assistance and follow-up counselling. Another one would prepare carefully selected people (not necesssarily young or with formal education) from villages for a particular trade and provide them with an entire package of training in technical, managerial, and entrepreneurial skills. It is too early to judge whether this experiment (or others that are being started elsewhere) will work. However, there is a great need and justification for a much wider exploration and repetition of this sort of experiment.

To help trainers and school teachers in this sort of effort, an experimental teaching material entitled "Understanding self-employment as a career" 35/ has been produced for the developing countries and is being tested by ILO. There are similar programs in industrially advanced countries. In Switzerland, for example, the Holderbank has a program in basic business economics called "Business in action." 36/ A group of Swiss firms periodically organize one-week seminars on business for teacher training colleges and for secondary schools. In this program, teachers are replaced by experienced practicing managers and a computerized business game plays a central role. The Holderbank is using these programs to help associate firms in developing countries to educate staff in basic business ideas and principles. However, the opportunities for adapting them to the needs and cultural environments of various developing countries and for using them in schools and colleges should be pursued much more vigorously then they have been hitherto.

Recent research on the state of the art in entrepreneurship development 37/ leads to three tentative conclusions. First, it is diffcult to distinguish the successful from the unsuccessful entrepreneurship development programs. Very few of them monitor the success of their own efforts (in terms of sales or profitabilty of their clients) and those that are successful are often more interested in doing a good job in their community than in publicizing their efforts internationally. Furthermore, the characteristics of successful programs are hard to quantify: they are usually described as flexible, inspired, and having committed, dedicated staff with good local contacts--all characteristics more likely to be found in many public agencies.

Second, the programs, successful and unsuccessful alike, focus on selecting their clients: they are continually seeking cheap and valid selection devices (such as asking a candidate to "sell me this pencil") but most often end up using complex and questionable selection aids. Selection is

vital bcause few people are entrepreneurs and the limited services of good
programs must concentrate on those few who are most likely to be able to
employ other people.

Third, all programs have difficulty deciding what they should do to
help and how to organize that help. Many of the better programs concentrate
on inspiring (through achievement motivation, for example) and on helping
entrepreneurs deal with their environment (the government, banks, customers,
and suppliers) and take advantage of support services. Such programs try, in
particular, to make the environment more supportive of entrepreneurship.
Generally, much more can be accomplished by removing barriers (most start-ups
get stopped trying to deal with the bureaucracy) than by teaching people how
to deal with unnecessary barriers. The main difficulty in organizing services
is one of "batching": businessmen have little inclination or time to sit in
classrooms; yet it is very expensive to squander efforts by providing one-on-
one services to thousands of individuals. Therefore, emphasis is often placed
on self-development materials and business clinics.

How to Make the Effective Approaches More Common

This part of the paper has provided examples of the best that we
could find in management development in developing countries. Although there
is much here to encourage us, we must admit that the best is all too rare--the
exception to the rule. How can we make the best today more common tomorrow?

First, we must always try to view management development as an
intervention system, the impact of which can be evaluated because no system
can evolve for the better without aiming for goals and without attempting to
measure progress toward those goals. True, evaluation is inexact and
difficult, but that is not a valid excuse for omitting it. As we have shown,
there are different levels of evaluation and each has its place, depending on

the type of the intervention. The critical problem today is that more than 90 percent of management development in the Third World is evaluated only in terms of participant time. It is important to move the higher levels of evaluation, and to emphasize performance improvement in client organizations as the ultimate result. This goal will provide incentives for management development professionals to acquire and use the more powerful tools at hand. An useful way to raise the expectations of clients is to publicize successes so that clients will become more aware of what is possible.

Second, clients with higher expectations must be willing to become partners in a difficult and often painful struggle. Less than 20 percent of public agencies and enterprises have budgets for management development. Publicity showing that management development pays dividends must also stipulate that it costs money. Having invested in manager development, many organizations will find that their people have become more valuable to others. Thus, they will have to solve many problems they were content to ignore before. Many will have to develop training policies alongside new, more appropriate career structures, merit systems, and fair performance evaluations.

Third, management institutions keen to foster more effective approaches and techniques may require help. Information must be circulated on what works and what does not; this information has to go beyond mere descriptions and must explain the causes of success or failure. For example, a great many workshops on training and for trainers are organized every year by different agencies. Yet workshops focusing on a critical assessment and popularization of new creative approaches to staff development are virually nonexistent. In some cases, a mere sharing of information may not be enough. Trainers from institutions as well as in-plant trainers in the public and private sectors may need more opportunities to practice approaches and techniques new to them, to become convinced about their advantages, and to become confident in using them. The international community can provide a great deal of help in this respect.

All in all, there is a great need to revitalize management education and training in developing countries and to make sure that this effort really addresses the priority problems of the practitioners. Courses that are run just for their own sake should not be encouraged. The determination to do things more effectively at institutions and in the public and private organizations served by these institutions will be the key factor in bringing about such a revitalization.

References

1. A. Tofler, The Third Wave (London: Pan Books-Collins, 1981), p. 328.

2. See also Economic Development and Private Sector (Washington, D.C., The World Bank, 1981); and J. Diebold, The Role of Business in Society (New York: AMACOM, 1982).

3. Revitalization of Basic Business Education at All Instruction Levels (Reston, VA: National Business Education Association, 1982).

4. On training and development experience of a range of multinational corporations operating in Asia, see The Asian Manager: Recruiting, Training and Retraining Executives (Hongkong: Business International Asia/Pacific, 1982).

5. See also S.R. Raveed and W. Renforth, "State Enterprise--Multinational Corporation Joint Ventures: How Well do They Meet Both Partners' Needs?" Management International Review, no. 1 (1983); and other references given in this article.

6. "Aramco's Incredible Training Bill," International Management, November 1981.

7. I. Serageldin and J. Socknat, "Migration and Manpower Needs in the Middle East and North Africa 1975-1985," Finance and Development, vol. 17, no. 4(19).

8. R.E. Berenbeim, Managing the International Company: Building a Global Perspective, Report no. 814. New York: The Conference Board, 1982.

9. Social and Cultural Factors in Management Development (Geneva: International Labour Office, 1966).

10. G. Hofstede, Culture and Management Development (Geneva: International Labour Office, 1983). A more detailed analysis appears in G. Hofstede, Culture's Consequences (Beverly Hills, Calif.: Sage Publications, 1980).

11. Cf. T.E. Deal and A.A. Kennedy, Corporate Cultures: The Rites and Rituals of Corporate Life (Reading, Mass.: Addison-Wesley, 1982).

12. See also R. Bennett, Management Research: Guide for Institutions and Professionals (Geneva: International Labour Office, 1983).

13. The most complete list is in M. Kubr and K. Vernon, eds., Management, Administration and Productivity: International Directory of Institutions and Information Sources (Geneva: International Labour Office, 1981).

14. See, for example, "Managing in Two Worlds," International Management, July 1981.

15. D.C. Korten, ed., Population and Social Development Management: A Challenge for Management Schools (Caracas: Instituto de Estudios Superiores de Administracion, 1979).

16. See also M. Kubr, ed., Managing a Management Development Institution (Geneva: International Labour Office, 1982).

17. See also D.C. Korten, ed., Management; D.C. Korten and F.B. Alfonso, eds., Bureaucracy and the Poor: Closing the Gap (Singapore: McGraw-Hill, 1981); and S. Paul, Strategic Management of Development Programs: Guidelines for Action (Geneva: International Labour Office, 1983).

18. See, for example, Opportunities and Priorities for Co-operation, Report of the Global Meeting on Co-operation among Management Development Institutions, Geneva, December 9-12, 1980, and Technical Co-operation among African Countries in Management Development (Geneva: International Labour Office, 1982. processed.

19. Three popular distillations of research on this topic are: R.T. Pascale and A.G. Athos, The Art of Japanese Management (New York: Simon and Schuster, 1981); W. Ouchi, Theory Z: How American Business Can Meet the Japanese Challenge (Reading, Mass.: Addison-Wesley, 1981); and T. Peters and R.H. Waterman, In Search of Excellence (New York: Harper and Row, 1982).

20. See reference 19.

21. See R. Abramson and W. Halset, Planning for Improved Enterprise Performance (Geneva: International Labour Office, 1979).

22. For example, the International Centre for Public Enterprises in Developing Countries (ICPE) uses a modified version under the acronym "Optima."

23. See, for example, African Regional Seminar on the Application of Appropriate Technology in Road Construction (Geneva: International Labour Office, 1980).

24. See Guide to the Training of Supervisors of Labour-based Road Construction and Maintenance (Geneva: International Labour Office, 1981); and Guide to Tools and Equipment for Labour-based Road Construction (Geneva: International Labour Office, 1981).

25. J.R. Adams and M.S. Kirchof, "Developing Project Managers: Adapting Training to an Organization's Needs," in Project Management Tools and Visions, Report of the 7th World Congress on Project Management (Copenhagen, 1982), pp. 15-21.

26. Managing Construction Projects: A Guide to Processes and Procedures (Geneva: International Labour Office, 1983).

27. See Results-oriented Maintenance Management Programmes: A Preliminary Report (Geneva: International Labour Office, 1982).

28. See, for example, Materials and Techniques for Co-operative Management Training (MATCOM) (Geneva:

29. Effective Computer Use in Developing Countries (Geneva: International Labour Office, 1980).

30. V.C. Patel, Identifying and Developing Indigenous Entrepreneurs: The Gujarat Experience (Ahmedabad: The Centre for Entrepreneur Development, 1982). See also V.C. Patel, "Innovations in Promoting and Developing New Enterprises." in Small Enterprise Development: Policies and Programmes, ed. P.A. Neck (Geneva: International Labour Office, 1977).

31. See "Xanadu--Mutual Help in Building Small Businesses," International Management, December 1982.

32. "Entrepreneurial Now," The Economist, April 17, 1982, pp. 47-52.

33. Guidelines for the Development of Small-scale Contractors (Geneva: International Labour Office, 1983), preliminary edition.

34. C. Relf, Helping Toward Self-reliance (Geneva: International Labour Office, 1982).

35. Understanding Self-employment as a Career: Teachers' Guide (Geneva: International Labour Office, 1981); experimental text.

36. "Swiss Multinational Acts to Bolster Private Enterprise," International Management, October 1982.

World Bank Publications of Related Interest

Accelerated Development in Sub-Saharan Africa: An Agenda for Action

In the fall of 1979, the African Governors of the World Bank addressed a memorandum to the Bank's president expressing their alarm at the dim economic prospects for the nations of sub-Saharan Africa and asking that the Bank prepare a "special paper on the economic development problems of these countries" and an appropriate program for helping them. This report, building on the *Lagos Plan of Action*, is the response to that request.

The report discusses the factors that explain slow economic growth in Africa in the recent past, analyzes policy changes and program orientations needed to promote faster growth, and concludes with a set of recommendations to donors, including the recommendation that aid to Africa should double in real terms to bring about renewed African development and growth in the 1980s. The report's agenda for action is general; it indicates broad policy and program directions, overall priorities for action, and key areas for donor attention. Like the *Lagos Plan*, the report recognizes that Africa has enormous economic potential, which awaits fuller development.

1981; 2nd printing 1982. 198 pages (including statistical annex, bibliography).

French: Le développement accéléré en afrique au sud du Sahara: programme indicatif d'action.
Stock Nos. SA-1981-E, SA-1981-F. Free of charge.

The Design of Development
Jan Tinbergen

Formulates a coherent government policy to further development objectives and outlines methods to stimulate private investments.

The Johns Hopkins University Press, 1958; 6th printing, 1966. 108 pages (including 4 annexes, index).
LC 58-9458. ISBN 0-8018-0633-X, $5.00 (£3.00) paperback.

Development Strategies in Semi-Industrial Economies
Bela Balassa

Provides an analysis of development strategies in semi-industrial economies that have established an industrial base. Endeavors to quantify the systems of incentives that are applied in six semi-industrial developing economies—Argentina, Colombia, Israel, Korea, Singapore, and Taiwan—and to indicate the effects of these systems on the allocation of resources, international trade, and economic growth.

The Johns Hopkins University Press, 1982. 416 pages (including appendixes, index).
LC 81-15558. ISBN 0-8018-2569-5, $39.95 hardcover.

Eastern and Southern Africa: Past Trends and Future Prospects
Ravi Gulhati

World Bank Staff Working Paper No. 413. August 1980. 24 pages.
Stock No. WP-0413. $3.00.

Economic Development Projects and Their Appraisal: Cases and Principles from the Experience of the World Bank
John A. King

The English-language edition is out of print.

French: Projets de développement économique et leur évaluation. *Dunod Editeur, 24—26, boulevard de l'Hôpital, 75005 Paris, France. 1969.*
99 francs.

Spanish: La evaluacion de proyectors de desarrollo economico. *Editorial Tecnos, 1970. 545 pages (including indexes).*
800 pesetas.

Economic Growth and Human Resources
Norman Hicks, assisted by Jahangir Boroumand

World Bank Staff Working Paper No. 408. July 1980. iv + 36 pages (including 3 appendixes, bibliography, and references).
Stock No. WP-0408. $3.00.

NEW

The Extent of Poverty in Latin America
Oscar Altimir

This work originated in a research project for the measurement and analysis of income distribution in the Latin American countries, undertaken jointly by the Economic Commission for Latin America and the World Bank. Presents estimates of the extent of absolute poverty for ten Latin American countries and for the region as a whole in the 1970s.

World Bank Staff Working Paper No. 522. 1982. 117 pages.
ISBN 0-8213-0012-1. $5.00.

First Things First: Meeting Basic Human Needs in the Developing Countries
Paul Streeten, with
Shahid Javed Burki,
Mahbub ul Haq,
Norman Hicks,
and Frances Stewart

The basic needs approach to economic development is one way of helping the poor emerge from their poverty. It enables them to earn or obtain the necessities for life—nutrition, housing, water and sanitation, education, and health—and thus to increase their productivity.

This book answers the critics of the basic needs approach, views this approach as a logical step in the evolution of economic analysis and development policy, and presents a clearsighted interpretation of the issues. Based on the actual experience of various countries—their successes and failures—the book is a distillation of World Bank studies of the operational implications of meeting basic needs. It also discusses the presumed conflict between economic growth and basic needs, the relation between the New International Economic Order and basic needs, and the relation between human rights and basic needs.

Oxford University Press, 1981; 2nd paperback printing, 1982. 224 pages (including appendix, bibliography, index).

LC 81-16836. ISBN 0-19-520-368-2, $18.95 hardcover; ISBN 0-19-520-369-0, $7.95 paperback.

The Hungarian Economic Reform, 1968–81
Bela Balassa

Reviews the Hungarian experience with the economic reform introduced in 1968 and provides a short description of the antecedents of the reform. Analyzes specific reform measures concerning agriculture, decisionmaking by industrial firms, price determination, the exchange rate, export subsidies, import protection, and investment decisions and indicates their effects on the economy. Also examines the economic effects of tendencies toward recentralization in the 1970s, as well as recent policy measures aimed at reversing these tendencies.

World Bank Staff Working Paper No. 506. February 1982. 31 pages (including references).

Stock No. WP-0506. $3.00.

Implementing Programs of Human Development
Edited by Peter T. Knight; prepared by Nat J. Colletta, Jacob Meerman, and others.

World Bank Staff Working Paper No. 403. July 1980. iv + 372 pages (including references).
Stock No. WP-0403. $15.00.

International Technology Transfer: Issues and Policy Options
Frances Stewart

World Bank Staff Working Paper No. 344. July 1979. xii + 166 pages (including references).
Stock No. WP-0344. $5.00.

Levels of Poverty: Policy and Change
Amartya Sen

World Bank Staff Working Paper No. 401. July 1980. 91 pages (including references).

Stock No. WP-0401. $3.00.

Models of Growth and Distribution for Brazil
Lance Taylor, Edmar L. Bacha, Eliana Cardoso, and Frank J. Lysy

Explores the Brazilian experience from the point of view of political economy and computable general equilibrium income distribution models.

Oxford University Press, 1980. 368 pages (including references, appendixes, index).

LC 80-13786. ISBN 0-19-520206-6, $27.50 hardcover; ISBN 0-19-520207-4, $14.95 paperback.

Patterns of Development, 1950-1970
Hollis Chenery and Moises Syrquin

A comprehensive interpretation of the structural changes that accompany the growth of developing countries, using cross-section and time-series analysis to study the stability of observed patterns and the nature of time trends.

Oxford University Press, 1975; 3rd paperback printing, 1980. 250 pages (including technical appendix, statistical appendix, bibliography, index).

LC 74-29172. ISBN 0-19-920075-0, $19.95 hardcover; ISBN 0-19-920076-9, $8.95 paperback.

Spanish: La estructura del crecimiento ecónomico: un analisis para el período 1950–1970. Editorial Teconos, 1978.

ISBN 84-309-0741-6, 615 pesetas.

Poverty and Basic Needs Series

A series of booklets prepared by the staff of the World Bank on the subject of basic needs. The series includes general studies that explore the concept of basic needs, country case studies, and sectoral studies.

Brazil
Peter T. Knight and Ricardo J. Moran

An edited and updated edition of the more detailed publication, *Brazil: Human Resources Special Report* (see description under *Country Studies* listing).

December 1981. 98 pages (including statistical appendix, map). English.

Stock No. BN-8103. $5.00.

Malnourished People: A Policy View
Alan Berg

Discusses the importance of adequate nutrition as an objective, as well as a means of economic development. Outlines the many facets of the nutrition problem and shows how efforts to improve nutrition can help alleviate much of the human and economic waste in the developing world.

June 1981. 108 pages (including 6 appendixes, notes). English. French and Spanish (forthcoming).

Stock Nos. BN-8104-E, BN-8104-F, BN-8104-S. $5.00.

Meeting Basic Needs: An Overview
Mahbub ul Haq and Shahid Javed Burki

Presents a summary of the main findings of studies undertaken in the World Bank as part of a program for reducing absolute poverty and meeting basic needs.

September 1980. 28 pages (including 2 annexes). English, French, Spanish, Japanese, and Arabic.

Stock Nos. BN-8001-E, BN-8001-F, BN-8001-S, BN-8001-J, BN-8001-A. $3.00 paperback.

Shelter
Anthony A. Churchill

Defines the elements that constitute shelter; discusses the difficulties encountered in developing shelter programs for the poor; estimates orders of magnitude of shelter needs for the next twenty years; and proposes a strategy for meeting those needs.

September 1980. 39 pages. English, French, and Spanish.

Stock Nos. BN-8002-E, BN-8002-F, BN-8002-S. $3.00 paperback.

Water Supply and Waste Disposal

Discusses the size of the problem of meeting basic needs in water supply and waste disposal and its significance to development in the context of the International Drinking Water Supply and Sanitation Decade. Examines the Bank's past role in improving water supply and waste disposal facilities in developing countries and draws conclusions for the future.

September 1980. 46 pages. English, French, Spanish, and Arabic.

Stock Nos. BN-8003-E, BN-8003-F, BN-8003-S, BN-8003-A. $3.00 paperback.

Poverty and the Development of Human Resources: Regional Perspective
Willem Bussink, David Davies, Roger Grawe, Basil Kavalsky, and Guy P. Pfeffermann

World Bank Staff Working Paper No. 406. July 1980. iii + 197 pages (including 7 tables, 2 appendixes, references, footnotes).

Stock No. WP-0406. $5.00.

NEW

Poverty and Human Development
Paul Isenman and others

Since economic growth alone has not reduced absolute poverty, it has been necessary to consider other strategies. The strategy examined in this study — human development — epitomizes the idea that poor people should be helped to help themselves.

Four chapters provide an overview of alternative strategies; a detailed look at health, education, nutrition, and fertility; lessons from existing programs; and an examination of broader issues in planning.

Oxford University Press. 1982. 96 pages (including statistical appendix).

LC 82-2153. ISBN 0-19-520389-5, $7.95 paperback.

NEW

Reforming the New Economic Mechanism in Hungary
Bela Balassa

Evaluates the reform measures taken in 1980 and 1981 (price setting, the exchange rate and protection, wage determination and personal incomes, investment decisions, and the organizational structure) that aim at the further development of the Hungarian New Economic Mechanism, introduced on January 1, 1968.

World Bank Staff Working Paper No. 534. 1982. 56 pages.

ISBN 0-8213-0048-2. $3.00.

NEW

Social Infrastructure and Services in Zimbabwe
Rashid Faruqee

The black majority government of Zimbabwe, coming to power after a long struggle for independence, has announced its strong commitment to social services to benefit the vast majority of the population. This paper looks at issues related to education, health, housing, and other important sectors and reviews specific plans and resource requirements to help improve the standard of living of the population.

World Bank Staff Working Paper No. 495. October 1981. 111 pages (including bibliography, map).

Stock No. WP-0495. $5.00.

Structural Change and Development Policy
Hollis Chenery

A retrospective look at Chenery's thought and writing over the past two decades and an extension of his work in *Redistribution with Growth* and *Patterns of Development.* Develops a set of techniques for analyzing structural changes and applies them to some major problems of developing countries today.

Oxford University Press. 1979; 2nd paperback printing, 1982. 544 pages (including references, index).

LC 79-18026. ISBN 0-19-520094-2, $34.50 hardcover; ISBN 0-19-520095-0, $12.95 paperback.

French: Changement des structures et politique de développement. *Economica, 1981.*

ISBN 2-7178-0404-8, 80 francs.

Spanish: Cambio estructural y política de desarrollo. *Editorial Tecnos, 1980.*

ISBN 84-309-0845-5, 1,000 pesetas.

Tourism—Passport to Development? Perspectives on the Social and Cultural Effects of Tourism in Developing Countries
Emanuel de Kadt, editor

The first serious effort at dealing with the effects of tourism development in a broad sense, concentrating on social and cultural questions.

A joint World Bank–Unesco study. Oxford University Press, 1979. 378 pages (including maps, index).

LC 79-18116. ISBN 0-19-520149-3, $24.95 hardcover; ISBN 0-19-520150-7, $9.95 paperback.

French: Le tourisme—passport pour le développement: regards sur les effets socioculturels du tourisme dans les pays en voie de développement. Economica, 1980.

49 francs.

NEW

Tribal Peoples and Economic Development: Human Ecologic Considerations
Robert Goodland

At the current time, approximately 200 million tribal people live in all regions of the world and number among the poorest of the poor. This paper describes the problems associated with the development process as it affects tribal peoples; it outlines the requisites for meeting the human ecologic needs of tribal peoples; and presents general principles that are designed to assist the Banks staff and project designers in incorporating appropriate procedures to ensure the survival of tribal peoples and to assist with their development.

May 1982, vii + 111 pages (including 7 annexes, bibliography).

ISBN 0-8213-0010-5. $5.00.

The Tropics and Economic Development: A Provocative Inquiry into the Poverty of Nations
Andrew M. Kamarck

Examines major characteristics of the tropical climates that are significant to economic development.

The Johns Hopkins University Press, 1976; 2nd printing, 1979. 128 pages (including maps, bibliography, index).

LC 76-17242. ISBN 0-8018-1891-5, $11.00 (£7.75) hardcover; ISBN 0-8018-1903-2, $5.00 (£3.50) paperback.

French: Les tropiques et le développement économique: un regard sans complaisance sur la pauvreté des nations. *Economica, 1978.*

ISBN 2-7178-0110-3, 25 francs.

Spanish: Los trópicos y desarrollo económico: reflexiones sobre la pobreza de las naciones. *Editorial Tecnos, 1978.*

ISBN 84-309-0740-8, 350 pesetas.

Twenty-five Years of Economic Development, 1950 to 1975
David Morawetz

A broad assessment of development efforts shows that although the remarkably successful in achieving growth, the distribution of its benefits among and within countries has been less satisfactory.

The Johns Hopkins University Press, 1977; 3rd printing, 1981. 136 pages (including statistical appendix, references).

LC 77-17243. ISBN 0-8018-2134-7, $16.50 (£8.00) hardcover; ISBN 0-8018-2092-8, $7.95 (£3.75) paperback.

French: Vingt-cinq années de développement économique: 1950 à 1975. *Economica, 1978.*

ISBN 2-7178-0038-7, 26 francs.

Spanish: Veinticinco años de desarrollo económico: 1950 a 1975. *Editorial Tecnos, 1978.*

ISBN 84-309-0792-0, 350 pesetas.

World Development Report

A large-format series of annual studies of about 200 pages, the *World Development Report,* since its inception, has been what *The Guardian* has called "a most remarkable publication. It is the nearest thing to having an annual report on the present state of the planet and the people who live on it." Each issue brings not only an overview of the state of development, but also a detailed analysis of such topics as structural change, the varying experiences of low- and middle-income countries, the relation of poverty and human resource development, global and national adjustment, and agriculture and food stability. Each contains a statistical annex, World Development Indicators, that provides profiles of more than 120 countries in twenty-five multipage tables. The data cover such subjects as demography, industry, trade, energy, finance, and development assistance and such measures of social conditions as education, health, and nutrition.

World Development Report 1982 *(See Publications of Particular Interest for description and sales information.)*

World Development Report 1981 *(Discusses adjustment—global and national—to promote sustainable growth in the changing world economy.)*

World Development Report 1980 *(Discusses adjustment and growth in the 1980s and poverty and human development.)*

World Development Report 1979 *(Discusses development prospects and international policy issues, structural change, and country development experience and issues.)*

World Development Report 1978 *(Disusses the development experience, 1950–75, development priorities in the middle-income developing countries, and prospects for alleviating poverty.)*

REPRINTS

Basic Needs: The Case of Sri Lanka
Paul Isenman

World Bank Reprint Series: Number 197. Reprinted from World Development. *vol. 8 (1980): 237-58.*

Stock No. RP-0197. Free of charge.

Brazilian Socioeconomic Development: Issues for the Eighties
Peter T. Knight

World Bank Reprint Series: Number 203. Reprinted from World Development. *vol. 9, no. 11/12 (1981):1063-82.*

Stock No. RP-0203. Free of charge.

Indigenous Anthropologists and Development-Oriented Research
Michael M. Cernea

World Bank Reprint Series: Number 208. Reprinted from Indigenous Anthropology in Non-Western Countries. *edited by Hussein Fahim (Durham, North Carolina: Carolina Academic Press, 1982):121-37.*

Stock No. RP-0208. Free of charge.

Latin America and the Caribbean: Economic Performance and Policies
Guy P. Pfeffermann

World Bank Reprint Series: Number 228. Reprinted from The Southwestern Review of Management and Economics. *vol. 2, no. 1 (Winter 1982):129-72.*

Stock No. RP-0228. Free of charge.

Modernization and Development Potential of Traditional Grass Roots Peasant Organizations
Michael M. Cernea

World Bank Reprint Series: Number 215. Reprinted from Directions of Change: Modernization Theory. Research. and Realities. *Boulder, Colorado: Westview Press (1981): chapter 5.*

Stock No. RP-0215. Free of charge.

WORLD BANK PUBLICATIONS
ORDER FORM

SEND TO:

WORLD BANK PUBLICATIONS
P.O. BOX 37525
WASHINGTON, D.C. 20013
U.S.A.

or

WORLD BANK PUBLICATIONS
66, AVENUE D'IÉNA
75116 PARIS, FRANCE

Name: _____

Address: _____

_____

Stock or ISBN #	Author, Title	Qty.	Price	Total

Sub-Total Cost: _____

Postage & handling fee for more than two free items ($1.00 each): _____

Total copies: _____ Air mail surcharge ($2.00 each): _____

TOTAL PAYMENT ENCLOSED: _____

Make checks payable: WORLD BANK PUBLICATIONS

Prepayment on orders from individuals is requested. Purchase orders are accepted from booksellers, library suppliers, libraries, and institutions. All prices include cost of postage by the least expensive means. The prices and publication dates quoted in this Catalog are subject to change without notice.

No refunds will be given for items that cannot be filled. Credit will be applied towards future orders.

No more than two free publications will be provided without charge. Requests for additional copies will be filled at a charge of US $1.00 per copy to cover handling and postage costs.

Airmail delivery will require a prepayment of US $2.00 per copy.

Mail-order payment to the World Bank need not be in U.S. dollars, but the amount remitted must be at the rate of exchange on the day the order is placed. The World Bank will also accept Unesco coupons.